中英文双语版

HOW MANY LIGHT BULBS DOES
IT TAKE TO CHANGE THE WORLD?

微妙的创新

［英］马特·里德利（Matt Ridley） 著

高李义 译

中国科学技术出版社
·北 京·

How Many Light Bulbs Does It Take to Change the World? By Matt Ridley/
ISBN:978–0255367851
Copyright © The Institute of Economic Affairs 2019
First published in Great Britain in 2019 by The Institute of Economic Affairs 2 Lord
North Street Westminster London SWIP 3LB in association with London Publishing
Partnership Ltd.
The simplified Chinese translation rights arranged through Rightol Media（本书中
文简体版权经由锐拓传媒取得 Email:copyright@rightol.com）

北京市版权局著作权合同登记 图字：01-2020-6278。

图书在版编目（CIP）数据

微妙的创新 /（英）马特·里德利著；高李义译 . —北京：中国科学技术
出版社，2021.4
书名原文：How Many Light Bulbs Does It Take to Change the World?
ISBN 978-7-5046-8879-8

I. ①微… II. ①马… ②高… III. ①技术革新—研究 IV. ① F062.4

中国版本图书馆 CIP 数据核字（2020）第 220337 号

策划编辑	申永刚 赵 嵘
责任编辑	杜凡如
封面设计	马筱琨
版式设计	锋尚设计
责任校对	邓雪梅
责任印制	李晓霖

出 版	中国科学技术出版社
发 行	中国科学技术出版社有限公司发行部
地 址	北京市海淀区中关村南大街 16 号
邮 编	100081
发行电话	010-62173865
传 真	010-62173081
网 址	http://www.cspbooks.com.cn

开 本	880mm×1230mm 1/32
字 数	115 千字
印 张	7
版 次	2021 年 4 月第 1 版
印 次	2021 年 4 月第 1 次印刷
印 刷	北京顶佳世纪印刷有限公司
书 号	ISBN 978-7-5046-8879-8/F·916
定 价	69.00 元

（凡购买本社图书，如有缺页、倒页、脱页者，本社发行部负责调换）

出版者的话

　　本书为畅销书作者马特·里德利撰写，他在《经济学人》杂志工作了八年，在《星期日电讯》和《每日电讯》开设了七年专栏。他曾出版过《毫不掩饰》《红色皇后：性与人性的演化》《基因组：人类自传》《自下而上：万物进化简史》《理性乐观派：一部人类经济进步史》等作品。他的书曾入围六大文学奖项。

　　为了读者可以更好地领略作者的原意，本书增加了英文原著部分，让读者在快速学习作者观点的同时，还可以领悟马特·里德利原汁原味的思想。

关于作者

马特·里德利（Matt Ridley）

马特·里德利的著作已被翻译成31种语言，销量超过100万册，并获得了若干奖项。这些著作包括《红色皇后：性与人性的演化》《基因组：人类自传》《理性乐观派：一部人类经济进步史》及《自下而上：万物进化简史》。马特·里德利于2013年2月加入英国议会上议院，并一直在上议院科学技术特别委员会和上议院人工智能特别委员会任职。他是英国纽卡斯尔国际生命中心的创始人。他还于2010年在《华尔街日报》上创建了"精神与物质"专栏，并在2013—2018年担任《泰晤士报》的专栏作家。

2014年，马特·里德利获得了经济事务研究所颁发的自由企业奖。他是英国皇家文学会会员和英国医学科学院院士，同时还是美国艺术与科学学院外籍名誉会员。

评论人

—— 斯蒂芬·戴维斯（Stephen Davies）——

斯蒂芬·戴维斯是伦敦经济事务研究所（Institute of Economic Affairs，简称IEA）的教育主管。1979—2009年，他曾任曼彻斯特城市大学历史和经济史系高级讲师。他还曾是位于美国俄亥俄州鲍灵格林的鲍灵格林州立大学社会哲学和政策中心的访问学者，以及弗吉尼亚州阿灵顿人文研究所的项目官员。作为一名历史学家，斯蒂芬·戴维斯于1976年毕业于苏格兰圣安德鲁斯大学，并于1984年获得该校的博士学位。他与奈杰尔·阿什福德合编了《保守主义与自由主义思想词典》，并为罗纳德·哈姆威主编的《自由意志主义百科全书》撰写过总论及若干词条。他还是《经验主义与历史》《财富大爆炸：现代性的本质与根源》的作者，并撰写过多篇文章和论文，主题涵盖公共产品的私人供给及犯罪和刑事司法史。

几乎每个小学生都知道托马斯·爱迪生发明了电灯泡，但他真的是唯一一个发明出电灯泡的人吗？如果他没有发明电灯泡，我们是否还一直生活在黑暗之中？

在2018年哈耶克纪念演讲上，马特·里德利解释说，事实上，还有其他二十多人都声称大约在同一时间发明了电灯泡。例如，1879年2月，约瑟夫·斯旺让电流通过真空玻璃泡内的一根碳丝，照亮了一间可以容纳700人的演讲室。8个多月后，托马斯·爱迪生提交了他的专利申请。大约在同一时间，来自英国、比利时、俄罗斯、德国、法国、加拿大和美国的发明家也制造出了玻璃电灯泡或者获得了制造玻璃电灯泡的专利。

这是一种被称为同步发明的常见现象。因此，虽然大众认为发明出电灯泡的发明家很伟大，里德利却认为基于当时的技术状况，电灯泡的问世是早晚的事。

里德利称，一个发明从创新到开发，最后到商业化，是人类社会一个重要的把控过程。我们依赖创新，但我们无法完全理解创新，无法预测创新，也无法引导创新。

他将这一点与哈耶克的论点联系起来。哈耶克认为，社会运转所需的知识分散在普通人之中，而不是集中于少数专家。

爱迪生说过一句名言：天才是1%的灵感加上99%的汗水。在解释这句话时，里德利提出了这样的观点：与所有进化系统一样，你无法轻易地催促创新。换句话说，我们不能在事物还没有准备好被发明之前就将它们发明出来。

他接着谈到了因自动化撤销的工作岗位多于其创造的工作岗位这一谣言，并讨论了创新如何促使经济增长。他还对最近流行的阻碍创新的例子进行了抨击，这些例子包括德国真空吸尘器行业、一些大型制药公司、英国国家医疗服务体系及欧盟采取的预防原则①。在谈到知识产权问题时，里德利认为，由于一些大企业的游说，最初旨在鼓励创新的专利和版权，更多地成了维护垄断者利益的方式。

他认为，创新是一个神秘而不被重视的过程。对于创新，人们进行的讨论太少，施加的阻碍太多，给予的重视太少。

伦敦经济事务研究所的斯蒂芬·戴维斯博士同意里德利提出的许多观点，但也提出了几点不同的想法。他指出，里德利认为，创新不是英雄般的远见卓识者或罕见的杰出人物的成果，而是大量普普通通、积极探索、勇于进取的人的成果，里德利这一论点与艾茵·兰德的观点相矛盾。在《源头》一书中，兰德的论点是：进步和创新来自普罗米修斯式的人物，人类的其他成员最终会追随他们，并从他们的创造力中受益。里德利的论点是：创新是一种社会现象，任何一项特定的创新都有许多开创

①　预防原则：是在科学认识尚不完善的情况下，应对可能出现的风险的一种战略。例如：纳米技术、转基因生物和内吸杀虫剂的风险。

者，其中的大多数人会被人们遗忘甚至不为人所知。对于创新，重要的是整个社会良好的贸易环境以及人们之间关于商品和思想的自由交换。

里德利认为，特定的创新在时机成熟之前不可能发生。戴维斯同样对这一观点提出了异议。他列举了历史上几个创新期和文明突然终结的例子，以此反驳"在持续创新方面（特别是18世纪以来的创新）取得的突破是不可避免的，或者说这是一个漫长的不断探索过程的结果"的观点。相反，他认为导致这种突然终结的力量和因素无法再次做到这一点。这些力量既包括人口数量少、人口密度低等自然原因，也包括限制贸易或获得土地等人为规则，这些规则原本是为了保护人们免受意外变化的影响，让生活更加可预测和稳定。这些规则的意外后果是，它们同时还妨碍和阻止了能使人们逃离马尔萨斯陷阱的那种持续创新。

里德利的结论是，既然创新是一个自下而上的进化过程，即源于分散的知识，政府就不应该胡乱地试图找到一个有关创新的神奇方法，而应该把重点放在消除阻止创新的事物上。我们还应该注意戴维斯的警告：在历史上，创新同样导致了限制和阻止变革与创新发生的善意反应和行动，并且不止一次地发生。

赛义德·卡莫尔（Syed Kamall）

伦敦经济事务研究所学术与研究室主任

英国特维克纳姆圣玛丽大学国际关系和政治学教授

致 谢

经济事务研究所感谢国际对冲基金（CQS）对2018年哈耶克纪念演讲和本书的慷慨赞助。

❦ 摘　要 ❦

- 创新是经济增长的一个非常重要的源泉。它通过释放资源用于其他活动从而增加产出的方式，提高生产率并创造财富。尽管创新具有重要的经济意义，但人们对创新仍不完全了解，也难以对其进行预测。

- 在现代社会之前，各种制度和做法都与创新背道而驰。这些制度和做法的主要目的是使生活可预测和更加稳定，并将变化的影响降到最低，但它们却阻碍或完全阻止了促使人们摆脱"马尔萨斯陷阱"的那种持续创新。

- 创新是贸易与交流的自然和必然结果。人们在见面时不仅进行物质商品的贸易，而且会进行思想和知识的交流，随后这些思想和知识会以新颖且意想不到的方式结合在一起。思想的交锋不仅仅是一种比喻，还是新思想如何产生并经过集体检验的一种表现。

- 技术创新是一种自下而上的现象，它是在普通人的想法中通过反复试验而产生的，而不是降临在少数聪明人身上的"神器"。它依靠的是中央规划者无法获得的分散知识。

- 主动挑选成功者是一个错误。政府倡导新技术的尝试长久以来都是失败的。政府与其试图找到一种有关创新的神奇方法，还不如把重点放在消除阻碍创新的事物上。

- 一些大公司为了防止竞争并维持自身的特权地位，经常企图扼杀创新。知识产权、职业注册（许可）制度和政府偏袒都将创新者拒之门外。

- 专利和版权已经成为保护垄断企业免受干扰的手段，这阻碍了通过复制和改进现有技术所进行的创新。这些专利和版权从某些方面使垄断企业通过垄断来获得财富和收入。知识产权以侵入性的方式限制实物商品所有者使用这些商品，日益损害了实物商品的不动产权。

- 虽然关注创新带来的意外后果是明智之举，但"预防原则"却被激进分子用来阻止新技术的应用，即使这些技术明显比现有技术更安全、更好。行动和不行动都会产生一定的风险。阻碍一项有可能带来好处的创新，可能会造成真正的伤害。

- 欧盟的监管引入了过度的预防措施、法律的不确定性、与其他法规的不一致性，技术法规、烦琐的包装要求及高昂的税费，阻碍了创新。英国脱欧后，英国政府可以决定采用"创新原则"以平衡预防原则。从本质上讲，这意味着，如果有证据表明政策将阻碍创新，就需要对政策重新加以审视。

- 通过缔约的贸易协定和欧盟等跨国监管机构来协调监管，存在扼杀政策竞争从而破坏创新的威胁。如果统治精英不再像弱小国家的统治者那样害怕竞争，那么他们遏制创新的动机将极其强大。目前，建立全球监管秩序的趋势有可能使创新停滞不前。

目 录 CONTENTS

第1章

改变世界需要
多少个电灯泡？

How many light bulbs does it take
to change the world?

马特·里德利
Matt Ridley

引言

◁◁◁◁◁◁◁◁◁◁◁

让我从一个悖论开始说起。这个悖论与电灯泡有关，是一个关于创新的老生常谈的比喻，因为电灯泡的发明在19世纪70年代算是一种创新。

悖论是这样的。没有人预测到电灯泡要来了，也没有人预料到它会被发明出来。然而，你越是仔细关注电灯泡的故事，就越觉得它被发明出来有其必然性。

罗伯特·D. 弗里德尔总结说，有21个人可以声称，他们在电灯泡首次亮相之前的几年里，不同程度地独立发明了电灯泡。考虑到他们中有两位至关重要的助手完成了一半的工作，所以我认为这一数字应该是23。

当然还有托马斯·爱迪生，他在1879年11月申请了电灯泡的专利。1879年2月3日，约瑟夫·斯万在纽卡斯尔的文学与哲学协会向700名观众展示了电流通过真空玻璃泡内的一根碳丝，将演讲室照亮的过程。

还有同样来自英国的威廉·罗伯特·格罗夫、弗雷德里克·德莫林斯和沃伦·德拉鲁，比利时的马塞林·约伯达尔，俄罗斯的亚历山大·洛德金，德国的亨利·戈培尔，法国的让·欧仁·罗贝尔–乌丹，加拿大的亨利·伍德沃德和马修·埃文斯以及美国的海勒姆·马克沁和约翰·斯塔尔，等等。

这些人中的每一个人都在爱迪生之前就产生、发表了玻璃泡内发光电丝的想法，或者就此想法申请了专利。这些玻璃泡有的是真空的，有的含有氮气，而且他们基本上都是彼此独立发明电灯泡的。

这是一种非常常见的现象，叫作同步发明。几乎每一项发明或发现，都会引发关于谁是最先发明者或发现者的争论。

事实上，电灯泡的故事不仅没有说明这位英雄发明家的重要性，反而告诉我们一个相反的事实：

创新是一个渐进的、递增的、集体的但又不可避免的过程。电灯泡不可避免地从当时的综合技术中产生了。考虑到其他技术的进步，它肯定会在该出现的时候出现，因为它已经成熟了。然而，仍然没有人预见到这一点。创新该如何既不可避免又不可预测地发生呢？

举一个最近的例子：搜索引擎。这可能是我一生中最有用的新工具，我几乎每天都会使用，我无法想象没有它的生活。比如，若没有搜索引擎，当我试图在书架上找一本我在准备这篇演讲稿时想要重读一遍的书时，我会感到沮丧。最后，我放弃了寻找，在我的Kindle（电子阅读器）上又一次买了这本书。

但是，我或者其他人是否预见到了搜索在互联网时代的巨大重要性？20世纪80年代，我们是否会闲坐着说："如果我们能有搜索引擎就好了？"不会的，就像17世纪的人们不会闲坐在一起说"如果我们能有蒸汽机，我们就能进行工业革命"一样。

然而，即使谢尔盖·布林从未见过拉里·佩

奇，我们还是会有搜索引擎，毕竟谷歌曾经有很多竞争对手。搜索引擎的发明者，就像电灯泡的发明者一样，都是完全可有可无的个体。当历史重新来过，如果他们这些人都不存在，其他人也会这么做。

我认为创新是整个人类社会最重要的悬而未决的问题。我们依赖创新，但我们无法完全理解创新，无法预测创新，也无法引导创新。

就这一点而言，值得对发明、开发和商业化加以区分，但我用创新一词涵盖这三个阶段。

这与弗里德里希·哈耶克有什么关系？我认为关系相当大。哈耶克在他那篇著名的关于知识在社会中的应用的文章中提出，社会运转所需的知识分散在普通人之中，而不是集中地提供给专家。在文章的末尾，他对著名的创新倡导者约瑟夫·熊彼特提出了批评。他谈的是我们确定如何最好地满足一个经济需求所需要知道的事实（哈耶克，1945），原文如下：

> 如果我们所有人都看到全部的事实，那
> 么问题就不会得到解决；如果这些事实仅为
> 一人所知……解决方案则会太独断了，相
> 反，我们需要搞明白的是解决方案是如何通
> 过每个都只拥有部分知识的人之间的互动产
> 生的。

哈耶克对进化论也很着迷。他对于我刚才提到
的关于进化论而非经济学的悖论的描述（哈耶克，
1973）如下：

> 如果能够查明过去对过去出现的特定生物
> 形式的选择起作用的特定事实，这将为现有生
> 物体的结构提供一个完整的解释；同样，如果
> 能够查明在未来某个时期对它们起作用的所有
> 特定事实，应该可以使我们预测未来的发展。
> 但是，我们永远也做不到这两点。

技术创新与进化一样，是一种自下而上的现

象，是在普通人的想法中通过反复试验而产生的，而不是降临在少数天才身上的"神器"。

在这个问题上我们太相信神创论了。长久以来，我们一直都说错了。我们把英雄挑选出来，讲述了一些有关灵感的故事，这些故事完全是误导人的：有人从浴缸里跳出来，有人被苹果砸中头部，有人看着水壶盖跳起来，等等。

谁发明了电脑？你越仔细研究，就越难以回答这个问题，并难以在约翰·冯·诺依曼、艾伦·图灵、约翰·莫奇利、约翰·皮斯普·埃克特、赫尔曼·戈德斯坦、约翰·文森特·阿塔纳索夫、霍华德·艾肯、格雷丝·赫柏、查尔斯·巴比奇和埃达·洛夫莱斯等某一位发明了电脑的说法之间做出决定。事实上，计算机是自己进化、出现并"发明"了自己。

谁发明了互联网？是每个人，但又不是某个人，互联网是在"进化"过程中产生的。英语也是一样：没有人发明，也没有人掌管，但它肯定是人为的。正如哲学家亚当·福格森在1767年说的那样，"人之行为的结果，但不是人之设计的结果"。

大多数情况下，创新是通过思想之间的某种重组而发生的，就像进化中通过基因序列的重组发生的基因变异一样。正如W. 布莱恩·阿瑟所言，每一项技术都是其他技术的组合，每一个想法都是其他想法的组合。胶囊相机是在一名肠胃病专家和一名导弹设计师隔着花园篱笆做了一番交谈后出现的。

这也一并解释了为什么我们会认为耗尽想法、资源枯竭或经济停止增长的观念是大错特错。正如我在《理性乐观派：一部人类经济进步史》（里德利，2011）中所说的：

> 知识最美好的一点在于它是真正无穷无尽的。哪怕从理论上说，也不可能耗尽思想、发明和发现的供给量。我持乐观态度最根本的原因就在这里。信息系统远比物理系统更为浩瀚，这是它的一个很美妙的特点。

> 概念的宇宙辽阔无边，让物质宇宙相形见绌。正如保罗·罗默（Paul Romer）所说，一块1G容量的硬盘能装下不同软件程序的数量，比宇宙原子的数量多2700万倍。

由此可见，正如爱迪生所说，创新主要靠汗水，而不是灵感。爱迪生和他的团队尝试了6000种不同的植物材料，用于制作电灯泡的灯丝，最后才决定用竹子来制作。换个角度来说，将一项发现或发明转化为可行的创新，远比一开始就有新想法要困难得多。

也许这可以解释技术史上的另一个规律：我们高估了一项创新在短期内的影响，却低估了它的长期影响。这就是在20世纪60年代以一位计算机先驱的名字命名的阿玛拉定律（Amara's Law）。

和所有的进化系统一样，你不能轻易地加速创新。我们不能在事物还没有做好准备之前就将它们发明出来。埃达·洛夫莱斯（Ada Lovelace）女士真不走运——你早出生了一个世纪。

极难想象有些东西在真正被发明之前几十年就可能已经被发明出来了。就连轮式旅行箱也是随着机场的普及和轻巧的轮子的出现，才恰逢其时地被发明出来。

摩尔定律告诉我们，计算机性能的改进是有规律可循的，也是可以预测的，然而我们却不能利用这些信息进行跳跃式发展。为什么不行呢？因为每一步都是下一步的必要条件，创新会朝着邻近的可能性发展。林奈乌斯说"大自然不会跳跃"，这是对莱布尼茨的回应。然而，我再说一遍，计划、预测或刺激创新同样出奇的困难。

史蒂夫·乔布斯将赌注押在计算机会成为消费品这个想法上，他是对的。但是，当伊丽莎白·霍姆斯试图直接效仿乔布斯的方法（以及他的黑色高领毛衣套装），把赌注押在血液检测产品上时，她以为只要她想要创新，创新就会到来，结果她主导了一起臭名昭著的Theranos（一家血液检测公司）欺诈案。

这里有两句名言可以提醒你，专家们在预测技术的未来时是多么的无力：

> 没有理由让每一个人家里都有一台计算机。
>
> 肯尼思·奥尔森（Kenneth Olsen），于1977年创立数字设备公司

> 到2005年左右，很明显，互联网对经济的影响不会比传真机更大。
>
> 保罗·克鲁格曼（Paul Krugman），1998年诺贝尔经济学奖获得者

当我还是个孩子的时候，未来的一切都是关于令人惊叹的新型交通方式：私人旋翼机、平常无奇的太空旅行、超音速客机。计算机几乎没有被提及，甚至还没有出现电话。然而，我几乎没有经历过交通工具的变化。波音747型飞机仍在大西洋上空飞行，它们是在20世纪60年代设计的。

　　相比之下，在20世纪上半叶，交通方式发生了巨大的变化，而通信几乎没有任何变化。我的祖父母出生在汽车和飞机出现之前，并在人类登月后去世，但在他们有生之年，电话、电报和打字机几乎没有发生什么变化。我的经历则截然相反，因此，并不是所有的创新都在加速。我有一种预感，未来50年不会像我们通常认为的那样，是关于计算机的，而是关于生物技术或其他东西的。

创新如何带动经济增长？

◁◁◁◁◁◁◁◁◁◁◁

现在，创新是大多数经济增长的源泉。但创新是如何带动增长的呢？这主要是时间方面的改变，经济增长就是减少满足某种需求所需的时间。

以人造光源为例，今天，为获取一个发光二极管（LED）电灯泡一个小时的光亮，你大约需要工作1/3秒；在1950年，你的祖父母需要工作8秒；在1880年，用一盏石蜡灯照明，需要工作15分钟；在1800年，用一支牛油蜡烛照明，需要工作6小时。这种时间上的减少，让你可以自由地将额外的时间用于赚取不同的服务或商品，或是放松和消费。

值得一提的是，创新没有任何导致整体失业率上升的可能性。如果你认为创新导致失业率上升，不仅无视了3个世纪里的证据，而且无视了理论。这是一种零和的收益递减思维模式。

自从农场里出现第一台脱粒机以来，人们就一直担心自动化会导致工作岗位流失。恰恰相反，自动化通过解放人力和资本来创造工作岗位，为人们相互雇佣寻找新的方式。

人类历史的重大进程是，我们的工作方式越来越专业化，使得我们的消费方式也可以越来越多样化。这一趋势在贫困时期发生了逆转，比如罗马沦陷后，甚至在美国的大萧条期，人们恢复了自给自足，记忆中充满了一家人在院子里养鸡种菜的故事。

与动物或自给自足的农民相比，大多数人可以用几个小时高度专业化的生产——一份"工作"——换取各种各样的食物、商品、体验、娱乐和旅行。我们为彼此工作。

由此可见，如果不能削减获取商品和服务所需的时间成本，创新往往就会失败。这就是核电、航天制造和可再生能源领域目前面临的问题。除非获得补贴，否则无法提供新的或更廉价服务的创新不会普及。

这也是为什么发明往往进展缓慢的原因：促进发明得以启动并改变世界的不是设备或想法，而是成本的下降。哈耶克说得很对，价格就是一切。

创新是科学的根源，创新也是科学的产物。蒸汽机导致热力学的建立，而不是热力学导致蒸汽机的出现。社交媒体、手机、无人机、区块链——这一切都不能归功于学术发现。大多数创新并非始于科学研究，有些创新确实是始于科学研究，但很多不是。

因此，增长是创新的成果。但什么是创新？为什么它会发生在我们身上，而不是发生在兔子和岩石身上？为什么它会在某些地方、某些时候发生，而不是在其他地方、其他时候发生？它是从什么时候开始的，又是为什么开始的？

对于最后一个问题，我仍然认为我的回答至少有一半是原创的，甚至所有想法都是原创的。我的回答是，在古人类历史上的某个时刻，不管是出于何种原因，他们开始交换，甚至把交换变成一种习惯，这就是创新的原因。当然，这有点循环论证的意味，但请耐心听我说。当人们开始交换东西时，思想便可以相遇和交融，结果形成了一种远比个人大脑强大的集体大脑。

我们知道，我们的祖先没有创新就拥有了技术，这听起来很奇怪。在近100万年的时间里，直立人在世界范围内制造的各种阿舍利手斧，其设计大致相同，几乎没有什么变化。

证据表明，尼安德特人虽然比直立人聪明很多，但也没有进行太多的创新。与现代人不同的是，当一种食物来源耗尽时，他们不会转向其他猎物，他们也不进行交换，他们只使用当地的材料制作工具。即使是最早的现代人类，也常常是通过贸易从很远的地方获取材料。我认为这不是巧合，没有交流就没有创新。简而言之，引发创新的正是贸易，而贸易大约有10万年的历史。

人类学家正在明白这一点。2011年，伦敦大学学院的一篇重要论文认为，在旧石器时代的非洲南部地区，新技术的暂时"爆发"能从人口统计学得以解释。也就是说，人口密度上升会导致创新的井喷；而人口密度下降则会导致技术的倒退。但种群密度对兔子没有这样的影响，因为在澳大利亚等国家，兔子泛滥成灾，其繁殖能力十分惊人，而兔子是动物，不会创新，只有人才会创新。因此，这表明交换和专业化存在因果关系。

米歇尔·A.克莱恩和罗布·博伊德（2010）此后在太平洋岛屿上找到了证据，证明任何岛屿居民在和其他岛屿居民接触前，其渔具的技术复杂性与人口规模和与其他岛屿的接触有关。最显著的例子是塔斯马尼亚岛，由于海平面上升，这里在一万年前变成了一个岛屿。此后，这里与世隔绝的岛民不仅没有从大洋洲大陆获得回旋镖等新技术，实际上反而倒退了，逐渐彻底放弃了骨制工具。

乔·亨里奇认为，上述事例表明，由于专业化，技术是一种集体现象，而不是个体现象。这是不切实际的理论。当然，来自现代世界的证据无可争辩地支持了贸易或交换与创新之间的联系。

我的朋友保罗·罗默（Paul Romer）因解决如何解释技术变革的问题，当之无愧地获得了2018年诺贝尔奖。这里有必要介绍一下相关经济学理论。大卫·瓦尔许在他那本名为《知识与国富论》的引人入胜的经济史著作中提出，亚当·斯密身上潜藏着一个矛盾，这个矛盾隐秘地低吟，两个多世纪以来基本上都被忽视了（瓦尔许，2006）。

亚当·斯密提出的"看不见的手"推动市场走向完美均衡，意味着收益递减或持平。与此不同，他提到的别针工厂则通过专业化和劳动分工表明了一个颠覆性的发现，该发现意味着收益递增。一个是负面反馈，另一个是正面反馈，到底是哪一个？

在亚当·斯密之后的几年里，大卫·李嘉图、约翰·穆勒（John Stuart Mill）、杰文斯、瓦尔拉、马歇尔和凯恩斯等经济学家基本上都忽略了收益递增和别针工厂。他们把注意力放在"看不见的手"上，近乎明确地估计，增长会随着接近均衡而放缓。以下是瓦尔许对约翰·穆勒的评论，例如：

> 穆勒并没有完全忽视技术进步，但他也没有试图对其进行解释——至少没有从经济角度进行解释。他简单地认为，这种情况至少会再持续一段时间。

然而，与收益递减相反的情况不断发生：增长加速。尽管如此，专业化和知识的增长从未成为经济学关切的核心问题。悖论时不时地浮出水面，需要神奇的思维对其加以解释，比如马歇尔的"溢出"外部性，瓦尔许将"溢出"外部性描述为一种巧妙的手段，它可以使不断增长的收益与有关"看不见的手"的完全竞争这一假设相符，并使数学结果仍然正确。

阿林·艾勃特·扬在1928年直言不讳地提出这个问题，他认为亚当·斯密忽略了这一点。别针工厂内发生的事情只是劳动分工的一部分："新工具、新机械、新材料和新设计的发明也涉及劳动分工"（瓦尔许，2006）。

约瑟夫·熊彼特也试图将知识和技术放在首

位，他表示，研究没有知识和技术的经济学就像戏剧《哈姆雷特》中没有王子一样。他坚定地认为增长的潜力是无限的，他写道：

> 最稳妥的预测之一是，在可预见的未来，我们将生活在食物和原材料匮乏的窘境中，把全部精力放在扩大总产出上，这样我们就知道该怎么做了（熊彼特，1942）。

但由于熊彼特是用文字而不是公式写的，他的观点在很大程度上被忽视了。

此后，罗伯特·索洛在1957年提出了令人震惊的结论：额外的土地、劳动力和资本只能支撑15%的增长（索洛，1957）。经济增长的其他原因一定是不断变化的技术。因为他是通过数学得出这个结论的，所以他的同事们最终注意到了这一点。

但在索洛的模型中，创新是一个外部因素，是一种从天而降的甘露。正如瓦尔许所说，"就像非洲地图一样，索洛关于增长根源的模型是由粗线条的轮廓组成，几乎没有内部细节，大多数有趣的行动都被刻意省略了"。顺便说一句，瓦尔许的书让我大开眼界。经济学家为何能在这么长的时间里持续忽视创新这一过去两个世纪最显而易见的事实呢？就这一点而言，今天的政治家又怎么能忽视创新呢？我作为上议院议员，观察到几个世纪以来这个机构一直无视创新，虽然它声称要解决这个国家的重大问题，但我可以用一只手数出我们讨论如何鼓励创新的次数。我们讨论得更频繁的是如何对创新进行监管。

罗默在1990年提出增长是内源性的，他认为，创新本身就是一种产品；知识既是经济的投入，也是经济的产出。新知识的关键特征有两点：它是非竞争性的，也就是说，许多人可以分享知识而不会耗尽知识；它具有部分排斥性，即谁最先掌握知识，谁就可以利用知识赚钱，至少在一段时间内是这样。知识的生产成本很高，但它可以自己收回这一成本。这正如瓦尔许所说：

> 人们为了赚钱而炮制新的说明书，然后要么对某些方面保密，或者申请专利加以保护；要么利用新发现的知识优势继续前进，创造更多的新知识。

在我看来，这是一个关键的见解，它削弱了左派的观点，即知识是一种公共产品，只能由国家支付费用；而右派的观点则是，政府需要以专利和版权的形式授权明确的垄断。如果设置得当，社会将在网络或市场中产生新的知识。

特伦斯·基利（Terence Kealey）进一步认为，证据有力地表明，私人利益集团会对研究进行投资，政府在假设市场失灵的情况下反而这样做，最终会排挤这种投资。我并不想在此参加这样的辩论，我只想说，无论是通过拨款、奖励、减税还是放松监管来鼓励研究，肯定都会有助于创新。

然而，主动挑选成功者是一个错误。在我的有生之年，政府一直在支持某些新技术，坦率地说，结果令人沮丧。协和式飞机、先进的气冷反应堆、互动电视、虚拟现实村庄、风力涡轮机、生物燃料——失败者的名单很长。我有一种感觉，石墨烯和电动汽车可能会加入这一名单。政府漏掉的成功者名单同样很长：互联网、手机、社交媒体、电子烟、页岩气、基因编辑。我们又回到了技术变革的不可预测性上。

创新的障碍

◁◁◁◁◁◁◁◁◁◁◁

　　我认为鼓励创新的秘诀非常简单，即找出并摧毁那些阻碍创新的障碍。因为总是有巨大的既得利益者在反对创新。正如弗雷德里克·埃里克森和比约恩·魏格尔（Bjorn Weigel）在他们的著作《创新的幻觉：这么多人这么努力怎么创造了这么少》中指出的那样，大公司和大型公共机构在竭力保护他们的寻租机会；他们竭力以各种方式扼杀创新（埃里克森、魏格尔，2016）。我举两个最近的例子：

　　詹姆斯·戴森爵士发明了无袋吸尘器。德国吸尘器行业游说布鲁塞尔，要求在没有灰尘的情况下测试真空吸尘器的功耗（为了防止全球变暖，要对真空吸尘器的功耗进行监管），因为如果周围有灰尘，德国吸尘器的效果就没那么好。2018年11月，戴森在法庭上打赢了官司，但这场官司耗时5年之久。其次，制药行业一直在大力游说——主要是在布鲁塞尔和华盛顿——对电子烟进行监管和限制，以保护其处方（尼古丁）贴膏和口香糖。

正如已故的卡莱斯图斯·朱马（2016）在他的《创新进化史：600年人类科技革新的激烈挑战及未来启示》一书中所记载的那样，在过去，伦敦汉森出租车运营商对雨伞的引入（当时英国人将雨伞视为一种禁忌，认为使用雨伞是种软弱的象征）进行了强烈谴责。1869年法国发明的人造黄油遭到了美国乳制品行业长达数十年的抹黑中伤。纽约乳制品委员会怒斥道："从来没有任何事物比这种人造黄油业务更蓄意、更骇人听闻的骗局。"到20世纪40年代初，美国2/3的州以虚假的健康理由完全禁止了人造黄油。

正如约翰·贝尔爵士最近指出的那样，英国国家医疗服务体系（NHS）是另一个因抵制创新而臭名昭著的"大企业"。它是西方世界最后一批采用质子束疗法治疗癌症的医疗服务机构之一。朗道是世界上基于蛋白质的血液诊断解决方案的领先生产商，总部设在英国，其产品销往145个国家，但该公司很难在英国国家医疗服务体系中立足。

科学界同样也充满了针对创新的障碍，比如同行评议及其对那些与所谓的"共识"相偏离的新想法进行惩罚的导向。最近的一篇文章详细描述了罗伯特·莫尔为了使他关于阿尔茨海默病和病毒的假说被人们认真对待所进行的长期斗争。莫尔的导师巴里·马歇尔为了研究胃溃疡在细菌学上的原因进行了更长时间的斗争。马歇尔最终获得了诺贝尔奖，但这是一项艰苦的工作。

经济学家亚历山大·塔巴罗克已经表明，通过增加研究成本和推迟药物引进，美国食品药品监督管理局在美国貌似合理地谋害了人民的性命，其数量比它所挽救的生命还要多。布林克·林齐和史蒂文·M. 泰勒斯（2017）在他们的新书《受困的经济：

强国如何致富、放缓增长和增加》中指出，知识产权、职业注册（许可）制度和政府偏袒也在很大程度上将创新者拒之门外。

专利和版权原本是为了鼓励创新，但现在更多的时候却成了保护垄断免遭破坏的方式。在迪斯尼公司的游说下，直到我死后70年，我的继承人都可以靠我的书赚取版税，这真是疯了。

还有就是预防原则。我们应该担心创新带来的意外后果——这个表面上合理的想法，已经演变成了一种手段，激进分子通过这种手段阻止拯救生命的新技术的启动，哪怕这些技术明显比现有技术更安全、更好。欧盟采用的预防原则对新技术的标准高于旧技术。例如，电子烟蒸汽中的化学物质种类比香烟蒸汽中需要检测的化学物质多得多。预防措施忽视了现有技术的风险，无视了减少危害这一概念。事实上，预防措施在本质上认为，你永远不应该尝试做任何新的事情。

凯斯·桑斯坦认为，当采取极端措施时，预防原则在很大程度上是没有意义的：行动和不行动都会对健康带来一定的风险，几乎没有理由在两者之间做出选择。预防原则的不对称性在于：在一个不完美的世界里，阻碍一项可能有益的创新会造成真正的伤害。这是弗雷德里克·巴斯夏关于"什么是可以观察到的，而什么又是不可以观察到的"这一理论的一种说法。

顺便说一句，欧盟委员会和欧洲议会对创新的敌意，是我在2016年投票脱欧的最大原因。看到欧盟委员会和欧洲议会坚决反对电子烟，反对（开采油气的）水力压裂法，反对基因改造，反对无袋吸尘器，而这往往是基于最虚假的理由，通常是在商业游说组织为了现有利益的要求下；看到欧盟给数字初创企业设置障碍，让欧洲处于数字革命的慢车道，没有任何数字巨头可与谷歌、脸书或亚马逊相抗衡；看到欧盟在《里斯本条约》中奉行极端版本的预防原则，我真的担心欧洲大陆今后无法发展。

2016年，欧洲商业组织编制了一份长长的欧盟监管对创新产生影响的案例目录。这份清单中包括两个监管刺激创新的案例（废物政策和可持续移动性），但更多的案例是监管因引入法律的不确定性、与其他法规的不一致性，技术法规、烦琐的包装要求、高昂的税费或过度的预防措施，从而阻碍了创新。例如，欧盟医疗器械指令大大增加了成本，从而减少了新医疗器械的供应。

英国在脱欧之后需要采取的是创新原则[1]，用以平衡预防原则。这是由欧洲风险论坛[2]提出的。实质上，创新原则指的是：评估每一项政策可能对创新产生的影响，如果你发现有证据表明该项政策会阻碍创新，那就重新考虑该政策。

2014年，来自世界上一些创新能力较强的公司的22位首席执行官签署了一封致让-克洛德·容克的信，要求他采用创新原则，马克·吕特在2016年荷兰担任欧盟轮值主席国期间也认可了这一原则[3]。当

---

[1] 创新原则。来自欧洲风险论坛。

[2] 创新原则——概述。来自欧洲风险论坛。

[3] 2016年3月3日，马克·吕特首相在欧洲商业日"改革促绩效"活动上的讲话。

然，人们对此充耳不闻。

因此，我要传达的信息是，因为创新是从分散的知识中衍生出来的自下而上的演化过程，所以政府应该把重点放在清除阻碍创新的因素上，而不是浪费时间试图寻找创造创新的神奇方法。

早在1662年，经济学先驱之一的威廉·配第就在其关于税收和贡献的论述中指出：

> 当一项新的发明刚开始被提出来时，每个人都表示反对，可怜的发明家则会胡思乱想，每个人都发现了他的几个缺陷，除非按照各自的方法进行修改，否则没有人会赞成。现在，100个人中没有一个人经得起这样的折磨，而那些经受住这种折磨的人，最终都会被别人的各种诡计所改变，以至于没有一个人能够自称是整体的发明者，也没有一个人能够同意他们各自在各部分中的份额。

今天，这一点比以往任何时候都更加正确。创新是一个神秘而又不被重视的过程。对于创新，我们讨论得太少，施加的阻碍太多，给予的重视太少。

Introduction

Let me begin with a paradox. It concerns the light bulb, that clichéd metaphor for innovation, which was itself an innovation in the 1870s.

The paradox is this. Nobody saw the light bulb coming. Nobody predicted its invention. Yet the closer you look at the story of the light bulb, the more inevitable it seems that it was invented when it was.

Robert D. Friedel has concluded that there are 21 different people who can lay claim to having invented the light bulb more or less independently in the years leading up to its debut. Given that two of them had crucial assistants who did half the work, I call it 23.

There's Thomas Edison, of course, who filed his patent in November 1879. But there's also Joseph Swan, who demonstrated to an audience of 700 people at the Literary and Philosophical Society in Newcastle on 3 February 1879 that he could illuminate a room—for his lecture—with an evacuated glass bulb containing a carbon filament, through which a current passed.

Then there is William Robert Grove, Fredrick de Moleyns and Warren de la Rue also in Britain, and Marcellin Jobard in Belgium, and Alexander Lodygin in Russia, and Heinrich Gobel in Germany, and Jean Eugene Robert-Houdin in France, and Henry Woodward and Matthew Evans in Canada, and Hiram Maxim and John Starr in America. And so on.

Every single one of these people produced, published or patented the idea of a glowing electric filament in a bulb of glass, sometimes containing a vacuum, sometimes nitrogen, and all before Edison, and they did so more or less independently of each other.

This is a very common phenomenon, called simultaneous invention. Almost every invention or discovery results in a dispute about who got there first.

The truth is that the story of the light bulb, far from illustrating the importance of the heroic inventor, turns out to tell the opposite story: of innovation as a gradual, incremental, collective yet inescapably inevitable process. The light bulb emerged inexorably from the combined technologies of the day. It was bound to appear when it did, given the progress of other technologies. It was ripe. Yet still nobody saw it coming. How can innovation be both inevitable and unpredictable?

Take a more recent example: the search engine. This is perhaps the most useful new tool of my lifetime. I use it pretty well every day. I cannot imagine life without it. I get frustrated when it's not available, as for example when I tried to find a book on my shelves that I wanted to re-read when preparing this lecture. In the end I gave up and bought the book again on to my Kindle.

But did I, or anybody else, foresee the immense importance of search in the era of the internet? Did we sit around in the 1980s saying 'if only we could have search engines'? No—no more than people sat around in the 1600s saying 'if only we could have steam engines, we could have an industrial revolution'.

Yet if Sergey Brin had never met Larry Page, we'd still have search engines. There were lots of rivals to Google. The inventors of the search engine, like the inventors of the light bulb, are all entirely dispensable individuals. Re-run the tape of history without all of them and somebody else would have done it.

It is my contention that innovation is the most important unsolved problem in all of human society. We rely on it, but we do not fully understand it, we cannot predict it and we cannot direct it.

It's worth at this point distinguishing between invention, development and commercialisation, but I am taking the word innovation to cover all three stages.

What has this to do with Friedrich Hayek? Quite a lot, I think. In his famous essay on the uses of knowledge in society, Hayek makes the argument that the knowledge required to make society function is dispersed among ordinary people, rather than available centrally and in concentrated form to experts. Towards the end of that essay, he takes to task Joseph Schumpeter, the famous champion of innovation. He's talking about the facts we need to know to determine how best to solve an economic need (Hayek 1945):

> The problem is thus in no way solved if we can show that all the facts, if they were known to a single mind ... would uniquely determine the solution; instead we must show how a solution is produced by the interactions of people each of whom possesses only partial knowledge.

Hayek was also fascinated by evolution. Here he is

describing the paradox I have just referred to, in regard to evolution rather than economics (Hayek 1973):

> If it were possible to ascertain the particular facts of the past which operated on the selection of the particular forms that emerged, it would provide a complete explanation of the structure of the existing organisms; and similarly, if it were possible to ascertain all the particular facts which will operate on them during some future period, it ought to enable us to predict future development. But, of course, we will never be able to do either.

Technological innovation, like evolution, is a bottom-up phenomenon that emerges by trial and error among the ideas of ordinary people, not a *deus ex machina* that descends upon a few brilliant minds.

We're too creationist about this. We've been telling

it wrong for a very long time. We've singled out heroes, and told stories about moments of inspiration that are thoroughly misleading: people jumping out of baths, people being hit on the head by apples, people watching the lids of kettles jump, and so on.

Who invented the computer? The closer you look into it, the harder it is to answer that question and decide between the claims of John von Neumann, Alan Turing, John Mauchly, John Adam Presper Eckert, Herman Goldstine, John Vincent Atanasoff, Howard Aiken, Grace Hopper, Charles Babbage and Ada Lovelace, to name just a few. In a real sense, the computer evolved, emerged and invented itself.

Who invented the internet? Everybody and nobody. It evolved. It's the same with the English language: nobody invented it and nobody is in charge. Yet it's certainly manmade. As the philosopher Adam Ferguson said in 1767, there are things that are the result of human action but not the execution of any human design.

Mostly innovation happens by a sort of recombination among ideas, very like the way genetic change happens through recombination of genetic sequences in evolution. As W. Brian Arthur has argued, every technology is a combination of other technologies, every idea is a combination of other ideas. The pill camera came about after a conversation over a garden fence between a gastroenterologist and a guided missile designer.

This incidentally is why the notion that we will run out of ideas or resources, or growth, is so wrong. As I put it in *The Rational Optimist* (Ridley 2011):

> The wonderful thing about knowledge is that it is genuinely limitless. There is not even a theoretical possibility of exhausting the supply of ideas, discoveries and inventions. This is the biggest cause for my optimism of all. It is a beautiful feature of information systems that they are far vaster than physical systems:

the combinatorial vastness of the universe of possible ideas dwarfs the puny universe of physical things. As Paul Romer puts it, the number of different software programs that can be put on one-gigabyte hard disks is 27 million times greater than the number of atoms in the universe.

It follows that innovation is mostly about perspiration, not inspiration, as Edison said. He and his team tried 6,000 different plant materials for the filament of a light bulb before settling on bamboo. To put it another way, turning a discovery or an invention into a workable innovation is far harder than having a new idea in the first place.

Perhaps this explains another regularity in the history of technology: that we overestimate the impact of an innovation in the short run, but we underestimate it in the long run. This is known as Amara's law after a

1960s' computer pioneer.

As with all evolutionary systems, you cannot easily hurry innovation. We cannot invent things before they are ready to be invented. Bad luck Lady Lovelace—you were born a century too soon.

It is surprisingly hard to think of things that could have been invented decades before they actually were. Even wheeled suitcases came at about the right time as airports expanded and lightweight wheels came along.

Moore's Law tells us that improvements in the performance of computers were regular and predictable, yet we could not use that information to jump ahead. Why not? Because each step was necessary for the next one. Innovation moves to the adjacent possible. 'Natura non facit saltus', said Linnaeus, echoing Leibniz. Nature does not jump. And yet, I say again, it's also surprisingly hard to plan, predict or stimulate innovation. Forcing it to happen is hard.

Steve Jobs took a gamble on the idea that computers

were ready to become consumer goods and he was right. But when Elizabeth Holmes tried explicitly to emulate his approach (as well as his black turtleneck outfits) with blood diagnostic tests, assuming that innovation would arrive if she demanded it, she ended up presiding over an infamous fraud called Theranos.

And here are two quotations to remind you of just how hopeless experts are at predicting the future of technology:

There is no reason for any individual to have a computer in his home.
Ken Olsen, founder of the Digital Equipment Corporation in 1977

By 2005 or so, it will become clear that the Internet's impact on the economy has been no greater than the fax machine's.
Paul Krugman, Nobel-winning economist in 1998

When I was a child, the future was going to be all about amazing new forms of transport: personal gyrocopters, routine space travel, supersonic airliners. Computers hardly got a mention, and telephones none at all. Yet I've lived through very little change in transport at all. Boeing 747s are still flying the Atlantic; they were designed in the 1960s.

By contrast, for the first half of the twentieth century, transport changed dramatically, communication hardly at all. My grandparents were born before the car or the aeroplane, and died after men landed on the moon, but saw little change in telephones, telegraphs and typewriters during their lives. I've had the opposite experience. So it's just not true that all innovation is speeding up. I have a hunch that the next fifty years are not going to be about computers, as we tend to assume, but about biotech or something else.

How does innovation cause economic growth?

Now, innovation is the source of most economic growth. But how does innovation cause growth? It's mostly about time. Economic growth is the reduction in the time it takes to fulfil a need.

So, to take artificial light as an example again, today it takes you about 1/3 of a second of work on the average wage to earn an hour of light from a single LED bulb. In 1950 it took your grandparents 8 seconds; in 1880, with a paraffin lamp 15 minutes; in 1800 with a tallow candle, 6 hours of work. That reduction leaves you free to spend the extra time earning a different service or good, or relaxing and consuming.

At this point, it's worth saying that there is no longer even a smidgen of possibility that innovation leads to an overall increase in unemployment. To believe that is to ignore not just the evidence of three centuries, but theory as well. It's to think in zero-sum terms of diminishing returns.

Ever since the first threshing machines on farms, people have worried that automation costs jobs. Instead it creates them by freeing people and capital to seek out new ways for people to employ each other.

The big theme of human history has been more and more specialisation in the way we work so we can get more and more diverse in the way we consume. It's a trend that goes into reverse during periods of impoverishment, when people return to self-sufficiency, such as after the fall of Rome, or even during the Great Depression in America, where memoirs are full of stories of families raising chickens and vegetables in the yard.

Compared with animals, or with subsistence

farmers, most people can exchange a few hours of highly specialised production—a 'job' —for a cornucopia of different foods, goods, experiences, entertainments and travel. We work for each other.

It follows that innovation usually fails if it does not cut the time-cost of acquiring goods and services. That is nuclear power's current problem, and space manufacturing, and renewable energy. Innovations that deliver no new or cheaper services don't spread unless subsidised.

This is also why inventions are often slow to get going; it's not the device or the idea, but the falling cost that helps them kick in and change the world. Hayek is right that the price is everything.

Innovation is as much the mother as the daughter of science. The steam engine led to thermodynamics not vice versa. Social media, the mobile phone, drones, block chain—all owe little to academic discoveries. It's just not true that most innovation begins with scientific research;

some does, but a lot doesn't.

So growth is the fruit of innovation. But what is innovation? Why does it happen to us, but not to rabbits and rocks? Why does it happen in some places and at some times, but not in others? And when and why did it start?

My answer to this last question, which I still think is at least half original, to the extent that any idea is original, is that there came a moment in the history of hominins, when for whatever reason they stumbled upon the habit of exchange, and that this was the cause of innovation. This is of course a bit of a circular argument but bear with me. When people began to trade things, ideas could meet and mate, with the result that a sort of collective brain could form, far more powerful than individual brains.

We know that our ancestors had technology without innovation, strange as that sounds. *Homo erectus* made Acheulian hand axes to roughly the same design all over the world for the best part of a million years with little change.

The evidence suggests that Neanderthals, though much more intelligent than *Homo erectus*, did not experience much innovation either: unlike modern people they did not switch to other prey if one food source ran out. They did not engage in exchange either; they used only local materials for tools, whereas even the earliest modern humans often sourced materials from a long way away, almost certainly through trade. I think that's no coincidence: without exchange you get no innovation. In short, what triggered innovation was trade. And trade is about 100,000 years old.

Anthropologists are catching on. In 2011 an important paper from UCL argued that temporary 'outbreaks' of new technology in palaeolithic southern Africa probably have a demographic explanation. That is, when population density rose, it resulted in a spurt of innovation; when population density fell, it resulted in technological regress. And since population density has no such effect in rabbits, this points to exchange and specialisation as the causal link.

Michelle Ann Kline and Rob Boyd (2010) have since produced evidence from Pacific islands that technological complexity of pre-contact fishing tackle on any island correlated with population size and contact with other islands. The most remarkable example is the case of Tasmania, which became an island 10,000 years ago as a result of rising sea levels. Thereafter its isolated population not only failed to acquire new technologies from the mainland, such as the boomerang, but actually regressed, gradually giving up bone tools altogether.

Joe Henrich argues that this shows that technology, because of specialisation, is a collective not an individual phenomenon. It's knowledge held in the cloud. And of course the evidence from the modern world overwhelmingly supports the link between trade, or exchange, and innovation.

My friend Paul Romer deservedly got the Nobel Prize in 2018 for his attempt to tackle the question of how to explain technological change. Here it is necessary to dip into economic theory. David Warsh, in his fascinating history of economics entitled *Knowledge and the Wealth of Nations* (the book I could not find on my shelf), makes the argument that there lurks a contradiction in Adam Smith that has rumbled underground, largely ignored for more than two centuries (Warsh 2006).

Smith's Invisible Hand drives markets towards perfect equilibrium, implying diminishing or flat returns. Smith's pin factory, by contrast, implies disruptive discovery through specialisation and the division of labour, which implies the opposite of diminishing returns—increasing returns. One implies negative feedback, the other positive feedback. Which is it?

In the years that followed Smith, economists such as David Ricardo, John Stuart Mill, Jevons, Walras, Marshall and Keynes largely ignored increasing returns and the pin factory. They focused on the Invisible Hand, more or less explicitly expecting growth to slow as equilibrium was approached. Here's Warsh on John Stuart Mill, for example:

> Mill didn't ignore technical progress altogether. But he didn't try to explain it, either—at least not in economic terms. He simply assumed that it would continue for at least a while longer.

Yet the reverse of diminishing returns kept happening; growth accelerated. And still, specialisation and the growth of knowledge never became a central concern of economics. From time to time the paradox would burst to the surface, to be explained by magical thinking, such as Marshall's 'spillover' externalities, which Warsh describes as 'a clever device to reconcile increasing returns with the assumption of Invisible Hand perfect competition and still make the mathematics come out right'.

The person who surfaced the issue most bluntly was Allyn Abbott Young in 1928, who argued that Smith had missed the point. What went on inside the pin factory was only part of the story of the division of labour: 'The invention of new tools and machinery and new materials and designs involved the division of labor as well' (quoted in Warsh 2006).

Joseph Schumpeter also tried to bring knowledge and technology to the forefront, saying that to do economics without it was like playing *Hamlet* without the Prince. And he was adamant that growth was potentially infinite, writing (Schumpeter 1942):

It is one of the safest predictions that in the calculable future we shall live in an embarras de richesse of both foodstuffs and raw materials, giving all the rein to expansion of total output that we shall know what to do with.

But because he wrote in words, rather than formulae, Schumpeter was largely ignored.

Then along comes Robert Solow in 1957 with his startling conclusion that extra land, labour and capital can explain just 15 per cent of growth (Solow 1957). The rest—the 'residual'—must be changing technology. Since he arrives at this conclusion using maths, at last his colleagues take notice.

But in Solow's model, innovation is an external factor, a sort of manna from heaven. As Warsh puts it, 'Like the map of Africa, the Solow model of the sources of growth consisted of bold outlines, with little interior detail and most of the interesting action deliberately left out'. (Incidentally, for me, Warsh's book was an eye opener. How on earth could economists have for so long continued to ignore innovation, the pre-eminent fact of the past two centuries? For that matter how could politicians ignore innovation today? I sit in the House of Lords, admittedly an institution that has defied much innovation for many centuries, but which purports to tackle the big issues of the country, yet I can count on the fingers of one hand the times we have debated how to encourage innovation. How to regulate it we discuss rather more often.)

It was Romer in 1990 who made growth endogenous, who saw that innovation was itself a product; that knowledge is both an input and an output of the economy, and that the key characteristic of new knowledge is that it is both non-rivalrous, that is to say lots of people can share it without using it up, and partially excludable, that is to say whoever gets hold of it first can make money exploiting it, at least for a while. Knowledge is expensive to produce, but then can pay for itself. As Warsh put it:

People cooked up the new instructions in the hope of making money, then either kept secret some aspects of them, patented them, or used the advantage of their newfound knowledge to keep going forward to create still more new knowledge.

This is a key insight that in my view undermines the view on the left that knowledge is a public good that can only be paid for by the state, and the view on the right that government needs to grant explicit monopolies in the form of patents and copyrights. Set up right, society will generate new knowledge within networks or markets.

Terence Kealey has gone further, arguing that the evidence strongly suggests that private interests will invest in research, and that government doing so instead, on the assumption of a market failure, ends up crowding out such investment. This is not a debate I want to join here, except to say that whether you encourage research by grants, prizes, tax breaks or deregulation, you almost certainly do help innovation.

Picking winners, however, is a mistake. Governments have championed certain new technologies throughout my lifetime, and frankly the record is dismal. Concorde, advanced gas-cooled reactors, interactive television, virtual reality villages, wind turbines, biofuels—the list of losers is long. I have a feeling graphene and electric cars may join that list. The list of winners that government missed is just as long. The internet, mobile phones, social media, vaping, shale gas, gene editing. We're back to the unpredictability of technological change.

Barriers to innovation

I think the recipe for encouraging innovation is terribly simple. Seek out and destroy barriers that get in its way. Because there are always huge vested interests ranged against innovation. As Fredrik Erixon and Bjorn Weigel have pointed out in their book *The Innovation Illusion*, big companies and big public agencies do their best to protect their rent-seeking opportunities; they strive to stifle innovation every way they can (Erixon and Weigel 2016). Let me give two recent examples:

Sir James Dyson invented the bagless vacuum cleaner. The German vacuum industry lobbied Brussels for the power consumption of vacuum cleaners (which were to be regulated to prevent global warming) to be tested in the absence of dust, because if there is dust around, the German devices work less well. In November 2018, Dyson won his case in court, but it took five years. Second, the pharmaceutical industry has lobbied hard— in Brussels and Washington mainly—for the regulation and restriction of vaping devices, to protect its prescribed patches and gums.

As the late Calestous Juma (2016) chronicled in his book *Innovation and Its Enemies*, in the past hansom cab operators in London furiously denounced the introduction of the umbrella. Margarine, invented in France in 1869, was subjected to a decades-long smear campaign (blame Professor Juma for the pun, not me) from the American dairy industry. 'There never was ... a more deliberate and outrageous swindle than this bogus butter business', thundered the New York dairy commission. By the early 1940s, two thirds of states had banned yellow margarine altogether on spurious health grounds.

The National Health Service is another big business that is notorious, as Sir John Bell has recently argued, for its resistance to innovation. It is one of the last health services in the western world to adopt proton beam therapy for cancer. Randox, the leading producer of blood diagnostics based on proteins in the world, is based in the UK. It sells to 145 countries, but struggles to get a foothold in the NHS.

Science too is full of barriers to innovation, such as peer review, and its tendency to punish new ideas that diverge from a cosy consensus. Consider a recent article detailing the long struggle that Robert Moir had to get his hypothesis about Alzheimer's and viruses taken seriously. Or the even longer struggle that Moir's mentor, Barry Marshall, had a generation ago to get the bacterial causes of stomach ulcers considered. Marshall got the Nobel Prize—eventually. But it was uphill work.

The economist Alexander Tabarrok has shown that, by increasing research costs and delaying drug introductions, the Food and Drug Administration (FDA) quite plausibly costs more lives than it saves in the US. Brink Lindsey and Steve M. Teles (2017) argue in their new book, *The Captured Economy*, that intellectual property, occupational licensing and government favouritism also do much to keep innovators out.

Patents and copyrights, originally intended to encourage innovation, have become far more often ways of defending monopolies against disruption. It is bonkers that, thanks to lobbying from the Disney Corporation, my heirs can earn royalties from my books till 70 years after my death. Let them get a job instead!

Then there is the precautionary principle. This superficially sensible idea—that we should worry about the unintended consequences of innovation—has morphed into a device by which activists prevent life-saving new technologies getting started, even when these are demonstrably safer and better than existing technologies. The precautionary principle (PP), as adopted by the EU, holds the new to a higher standard than the old. E-cigs have to test their vapour for far more chemicals than cigarettes have to, for example. It ignores the risks of existing technologies, defying the concept of harm reduction. Indeed, it essentially argues that you should never do anything for the first time.

Cass Sunstein argues that when taken to an extreme, the precautionary principle is largely meaningless: both action and inaction create some risk to health, leaving little reason to choose between the two. The asymmetric nature of the PP is this: in an imperfect world, standing in the way of an innovation that might do good causes real harm. It's a version of Frédéric Bastiat's argument about the seen and the unseen.

Hostility to innovation in the European Commission and Parliament, by the way, is the biggest reason I voted Leave in 2016. Having seen the Commission and Parliament set their faces against vaping, against fracking, against genetic modification, against bagless vacuum cleaners, often on the most spurious of grounds and often at the behest of corporate lobbies for incumbent interests; having seen the way the EU placed obstacles in the way of digital start-ups, leaving Europe in the slow lane of the digital revolution, and with no digital giants to rival Google, Facebook or Amazon; and having watched the EU's entrenching of an extreme version of the precautionary principle in the Lisbon Treaty itself, I am really worried that this continent won't be able to grow in the future.

In 2016, BusinessEurope produced a long catalogue of cases in which EU regulation had affected innovation. The list includes two cases where regulation stimulated innovation (waste policies and sustainable mobility), but far more where it hampered change by introducing legal uncertainty, inconsistency with other regulations, technology-prescriptive rules, burdensome packaging requirements, high compliance costs or excessive precaution. For example, the EU medical devices directive has greatly increased the cost and reduced the supply of new medical devices.

What Britain needs to adopt in the wake of Brexit is the innovation principle[1] to balance the precautionary principle. This was proposed by the European Risk Forum.[2] In essence, it says: examine every policy for the impact it could have on innovation, and if you find evidence that the policy is going to impede it, then rethink it.

Twenty-two chief executives from some of the world's more innovative companies signed a letter to Jean-Claude Juncker in 2014 asking him to adopt the innovation principle, and the Dutch Prime Minister, Mark Rutte, endorsed it during his country's presidency of the EU in 2016.[3] That fell on deaf ears, of course.

So my message is that because innovation is a

[1] Innovation Principle. European Risk Forum.
[2] The Innovation Principle—overview. European Risk Forum.
[3] Toespraak van minister-president Rutte bij het Business Europe Day 'Reform to Perform' event, 3 March 2016.

bottom-up evolutionary process deriving from dispersed knowledge, instead of messing around trying to find a magic way to create innovation, government should focus on removing things that stop it.

As long ago as 1662 William Petty, one of the pioneers of economics, pointed out in his treatise on taxes and contributions that:

When a new invention is first propounded in the beginning every man objects and the poor inventor runs the gantloop of all petulant wits, every man finding his several flaw, no man approving it unless mended according to his own device. Now, not one of a hundred outlives this torture, and those that do are at length so changed by the various contrivances of others, that not any one man can pretend to the invention of the whole, nor well agree about their respective share in the parts.

Today, this is more true than ever. Innovation is a mysterious and under-appreciated process that we discuss too rarely, hamper too much and value too little.

参考文献
References

[1] Erixon, F. and Weigel, B. (2016) *The Innovation Illusion: How So Little Is Created by So Many Working So Hard*. Yale University Press.

[2] Hayek, F. A. (1945) The use of knowledge in society. *American Economic Review* 35(4): 519–30.

[3] Hayek, F. A. (1973) *Law, Legislation and Liberty*, Vol. 1: *Rules and Order*. London: Routledge and Kegan Paul.

[4] Juma, C. (2016) *Innovation and Its Enemies: Why People Resist New Technologies*. Oxford University Press.

[5] Kline, M. A. and Boyd, R. (2010) Population size predicts technological complexity in Oceania. *Proceedings of the Royal Society B: Biological Sciences* 277(1693): 2559–64.

[6] Lindsey, B. and Teles, S. (2017) *The Captured Economy: How the Powerful Become Richer, Slow Down Growth, and Increase Inequality*. Oxford University Press.

[7] Petty, W. (1662) *A Treatise of Taxes and Contributions*. London: N. Brooke.

[8] Ridley, M. (2011) *The Rational Optimist: How Prosperity Evolves*. London: 4th Estate.

[9] Schumpeter, J. (1942) *Capitalism, Socialism and Democracy*. New York: Harper & Brothers.

[10] Solow, R. M. (1957) Technical change and the aggregate production function. *Review of Economics and Statistics* 39(3): 312–20.

[11] Warsh, D. (2006) *Knowledge and the Wealth of Nations: A Story of Economic Discovery*. New York: W. W. Norton and Company.

第 2 章

问题与讨论

Questions and discussion

圆桌讨论

◁◁◁◁◁◁◁◁◁◁◁◁

查尔斯·阿莫斯：

> 在你看来，为了最大限度地激发创新，你会取消哪一项具体的监管？

马特·里德利：

> 可能是预防原则，或者更确切地说，我会在预防原则和创新原则之间取得平衡。我会淡化预防原则，因为我认为它确实造成了真正的问题。例如，在转基因食品方面，我们现在知道，我们错过了在农业经济和农业生态领域的重大进步，因为这些进步减少了全世界化学品的使用。然而，

71

欧洲无法取得这样的进步，我们与其失之交臂，所以我会选择预防原则。

胡里欧·亚历杭德罗：

我与利伯兰、比特国，一些人工智能、区块链以及像海洋家园研究所这样的"共识社区"合作。在金融、商业、创意交易与交流领域，已经有许多创新，政府等中央机构内部却很少有创新，但也有一个物理场所，让个人能够相互联系。这就是我们所说的共识社区，也被称为私人城市，或特许城市、智能城市。你会不会认为这可能是一种新的未来的进化？不是从数字方面，实际上是在物理方面，如何让人们自由地相互交流，而不是像区块链或人工智能的可预测性那样创造数字交易？

马特·里德利：

这是一个有趣的观点。当然，保罗·罗默

是特许城市理念的拥护者，他认为，你应该对世界上某个地方的一个贫穷国家说，"我们能不能拥有你的一块土地，我们能不能在那里建立一个自由贸易城市？"

我认为这是一个很不错的想法，但我认为这永远都不会发生，因为，不到迫不得已的时候，没有一个国家会为了实现这个目标而交出自己的一大块领土。保罗一度有这样一个想法，他可以在关塔那摩湾做这件事，对我而言，这听起来是一个相当不错的主意。

PayPal[1]公司的创始人彼得·泰尔指出，在过去十年左右的时间里，大多数创新都发生在数字经济而不是实体经济中，原因之一是数字创新是无须许可的，而实体的东西则不是。我们基本上还没来得及给比特币的创新设置障碍，我们所有的障碍都与

---

[1] PayPal：是一个总部位于美国加利福尼亚州圣荷西市的互联网第三方支付服务商，允许在使用电子邮件来标识身份的用户之间转移资金，避免了传统的邮寄支票或者汇款的方法。

原子的创新有关。

当然，这种情况正在改变。政府正开始打压比特币，可以说，目前打压的速度相当快，但我认为这是一个有趣的观点。目前，我们认为创新在很大程度上是一种数字化的东西：人工智能、区块链、社交媒体，所有这些东西，对于上一代人来说，都是真的。但这可能是因为我们让实体世界的创新变得更加困难了，这并不是说实体世界没有创新，实际上实体世界的创新已经相当多了。

约翰·威尔顿·休斯：

尤其是对于在场的年轻人，你们能不能举几个例子，比如说，从自己非常丰富的科研经历中举例——我知道冷港（地名，美国南北战争期间曾在此发生过著名的冷港战役）和其他地方——你们真的认为创新可以很顺利地进行，并且可以很快地转化吗？还是只是为了鼓励一下大家？

马特·里德利：

这是一个关于创新已经或可以被顺利引入的例子。这取决于你所说的顺利是什么意思，我在演讲中曾多次使用抽电子烟和电子烟作为案例史。为什么在英国抽电子烟的人比其他所有欧洲国家多出约2.5倍，为什么澳大利亚仍然禁止电子烟，但英国却不禁止，这是一个非常有趣的问题。为什么电子烟在美国正迎头赶上，而英国却遥遥领先。英国有一个多样化的电子烟产业。越来越多的吸烟者开始吸电子烟。在英国，吸烟率下降得更快。日本人采用了一种不同的技术，即加热却不燃烧的香烟，而且带电子烟入境在日本仍然是非法的。我回忆起一次幸运的意外，在联合政府执政早期，政府和行为洞察力小组（又称"助推小组"）的负责人戴维·哈尔彭，遇到了他的老朋友罗里·萨瑟兰，这位广告业高管是电子烟的早期使用者，他告诉戴维·哈尔彭这些东西是什么，哈尔彭认为，“这很有趣。这些东西实际上有助于减少吸烟现象，而不是让问题变得更糟。”

哈尔彭给戴维·卡梅伦写了一份备忘录——在这个故事中每个人都叫戴维——故事的大意是“当公共卫生专家进门告诉你要禁止这种东西时，你要抵制他们，因为这可能是一项好的技术，而非一项糟糕的技术”。

但后来它与欧盟的《烟草产品指令》纠缠在了一起，该指令禁止电子烟广告，也拖慢了这个国家的戒烟速度。所以，障碍一直存在，但这仍是一个推动创新的例子。

另一个例子是英国的线粒体替代疗法，这同样是一项治疗一种特别罕见疾病的精湛科学。该疗法被提交给了议会，我们在议会两院为此进行了激烈的辩论。两院均以压倒性多数通过了这一疗法，该疗法得以继续推进。然后，由于各种技术问题，该疗法花了较长的时间才开始施行，但并不是因为有人反对。所以，推动创新是可以做到的。

问题解答

◁◁◁◁◁◁◁◁◁◁◁

提问者1：你将如何应对未来可能限制人类自由的基因增强？

马特·里德利：

通过基因工程限制人类自由，这会有什么风险？又会有什么前景？到目前为止，生殖技术和基因技术一直在给我们提供更多可能。比如体外受精，即试管婴儿技术。人们曾经认为，这会成为想要培养超人的"独裁者"们的工具。在20世纪60年代和70年代，人们对此真的非常担心，如果体外受精流行起来，变得十分容易操作，人们会利用它来将每个人变成社会精英的后代，等等。

事实上，体外受精产生了完全相反的效果。它让那些不能生育的人能够拥有自己的孩子，这项技术帮助了他们。而对诺贝尔奖获得者精子的需求被证明是非常小的，因为人们不想让诺贝尔奖获得者做他们孩子的父亲，他们想要的是自己的孩子。你知道，他们希望孩子和自己一样。因此，我认为，如果我们在设计婴儿类型的技术方面取得任何进展，也会发生同样的情况。

我估计人们的需求会像现在这样，通过胚胎植入子宫前的基因筛查手段来解决问题。这么做是为了消除疾病风险，而不是改善和提升。因此，我对人们将如何使用这些技术是不会过于担心的，当然我说的是在限制人类自由方面。

罗伯特·科博尔德：

我坚定地认为，我们需要消除创新所面临

的障碍。我想知道，我们是否需要将这一
见解拓展到经历了一系列可识别阶段的人
类意识领域？整体理论的一个重要见解
是，我们已经从传统的责任和价值观阶
段，到达现代主义的经济增长和世俗价值
观阶段，到了后现代阶段。我们怎样才能
把这一见解融入自己的个性中去？我们如
何才能在自己的进化过程中消除创新面临
的障碍，就像在技术的进化过程中一样？

马特·里德利：

总的来说，我不得不承认，我还没有真正
考虑过这个问题。我认为，我们现在所进
行的文化、经济和技术进化的数量和速度
都已经十分惊人，所以我对于改变我们的
生物学特性并不太担心。当然，我们确实
已经改变了自身的生物学特性，已经适应
了现代生活。

理查德·弗朗汉姆刚刚出版了一本引人入

胜的书，该书讲述了我们如何成为一个被
驯化的物种。我们学会了聚集在一起，而
不互相攻击，这一点是黑猩猩做不到的。
如果我们是黑猩猩的话，这个房间将会一
片混乱。我们通过选择即进化的形式成为
被驯化的物种。

我真的认为，我们已经把大部分责任推给
了技术进化，浪费时间试图鼓励我们物种
的生物进化是没有意义的，因为它作为一
种改变的方式太过缓慢和不充分。

乔纳森·克拉克：

那么，我们是否应该废除不列颠学会和英国
皇家学会这两个除了成为保护主义者对创新
进行限制之外没有其他功能的著名机构？

马特·里德利：

好吧，既然这两个机构都没有推选我成为
它们的成员，我完全同意。

露西·内维尔·罗尔夫：

> 鉴于你所说的创新的扩散过程，我想让你暂时担任财政大臣，告诉我们你对诸如研发税收抵免等创新激励措施的看法。

提问者2：我的问题实际上是相似的。几年前，政府进行了一次"耐心资本审议"。我的问题是，您认为没有耐心的投资者在多大程度上抑制了创新？

马特·里德利：

> 嗯，我认为对于露西的问题以及第二个问题，我的回答可能非常相似，因为我喜欢任何鼓励研究和开发的东西，只要它不是试图挑选成功者或者给予特殊对待就行，我担心弹射器（用以从舰船上弹射飞机升空）和这方面的东西。虽然他们在那里还不算太差，但我确实认为，在这个国家，我们在第二阶段，即耐心资本、积累和商业化方面，长期表现不佳。而我们仍然认

为创新是发明、发现，实际上，创新是爱迪生所说的1%的灵感，而不是99%的汗水。源于这些想法的激励企业发展的措施，可能是英国人需要关注的地方，从而克服我们在这方面固有的问题。所以，我完全支持耐心资本，像企业家投资获利减免和企业投资计划确实都产生了很大的影响。

英国的创业生态系统实际上相当壮观：自2010年以来，每年有60万家创业公司，比欧盟其他国家的总和还要多，远远超过了10年前的规模。现在，其中一些企业可能境况不佳，但企业家投资获利减免和企业投资计划有利于第二阶段工作的更好开展，我们需要在此基础上再接再厉，让它在以后继续发挥作用。

提问者3：您之前提出，您把对创新的敌意和预防原则作为投票脱欧的理由，我的问题是，考虑到目前英国脱欧谈判的气氛，特别是首相特雷莎·梅新起草的协议，英国在退出欧盟后拥抱创新的可能性有多大？

马特·里德利：

这让我想到了如何鼓励欧盟以外的创新，如果我们真的在欧盟以外的话，以及我们即将从英国政府发表的协议上听到的内容具有明显的高度一致性。

特别是对商品的高度一致性将让人很难有不同的做法。就拿基因编辑来说，世界上其他国家都说这项技术不需要进行严格而具体的监管，欧洲法院却裁定确实需要严格而具体的监管，因此，这项技术正在以最快的速度离开这个国家，前往加拿大和其他地方。我说的是农业领域的基因编辑。当涉及医学领域的基因编辑时，情况会有所不同。

如果我们离开欧盟，我希望我们能做的事情之一就是说："好的。如果英国脱欧，我们将认识到基因编辑需要较少的监管，可以快速投入生产。"在各项协议下，我们将很难接受英国脱欧在这一方面的内容，我不否认这一点。

约翰·德·斯塔福德：

哈耶克在《通往奴役之路》一书中写道：当存在无数监管时，这条道路的尽头就是极权主义国家、暴政和独裁。在英国和欧洲，我可以看到这条道路的尽头。普通人如何才能用创新来扭转这一前进方向呢？

马特·里德利：

我们如何利用创新绕过向极权主义国家的转变？我们认为从传真机、手机开始一直到互联网，这些技术的出现，会给个人带来不可思议的解放，会破坏国家对我们的控制基础，这不是很吸引人吗？

20年前，我们对这件事太理想化了。现在几乎很难记起当初的情况。国家已经反击，并找到了利用这些技术的方法，无论是通过假新闻还是通过监控，或者其他什么方式，让我们和以前一样受到他们的控制，在某些情况下可能会是更多的监控。然而，这些事情接连不断，我确实认为将会有机会通过技术来化解极权主义国家的力量，总体来说，妖怪已经从瓶子里出来了。在西方民主国家建立一个绝对的极权主义国家会相对困难，但我不得不说，近年来其他一些国家证明这出乎意料的容易，这让我大吃一惊。

提问者4：我记得您之前在讲座中谈到，美国食品药品监督管理局通过挑选成功者，经过20年的审批过程，可能造成了弊大于利。显然，在我看来，这是为了防止政客卖给你一种他声称能治愈你的癌症的"天降神药"。所以，我想问，您认为平衡事前测试系统和专门针对欺诈者的事后系统的最佳方式是什么？或者说，您认为这些恐惧被夸大了吗？

马特·里德利:

我觉得我不是美国食品药品监督管理局和医疗法规方面的专家，不能在这里给你一个非常全面的回答。很明显，我们不希望出现另一起"反应停"（Thalidomide，学名沙利度胺，原用作妊娠妇女的镇静药，但在20世纪60年代因发现会引起胎儿四肢畸形而被禁用）事件，我们需要在新药物进入人体之前进行测试，等等。但同时，我们必须鼓励新想法和新技术的出现，我觉得目前我们还没有找到合适的平衡点。

如果你关注制药公司把从专利中获得的垄断利润用在了什么地方，你会发现，不一定是研发，基本上是营销，大量的营销，所以这也在强化垄断。我认为这个问题需要得到解决。

存在允许"孤儿药"（又称为"罕见药"，用以预防、治疗、诊断罕见病的药品）在不同条件下进行测试这样的事情；允许垂死的人尝试药物，让他们贡献关于药物安

全性的知识，等等；有各种各样富有想象
力的方法可以尝试。

罗伯特·阿菲亚：

我本以为，竞争是创新的重要源泉。那么，
通过鼓励竞争，难道你不会得到更多的创
新吗？

马特·里德利：

竞争是绝对的，但我有时认为自由市场的
人谈论竞争谈得太多了，而合作太少了。
实际上，市场中纵向发生的是买家和卖家
之间的合作，而两个卖家之间的横向竞争
是非常重要的，这是其中至关重要的一
部分。但我觉得，如果我们过多地谈论这
些，而不谈论在这种世界中人们相互合作
的方式，就会让人望而却步。
我认为，与自己竞争，为客户提供更好的
产品，就像与他人竞争一样重要。

Round-table discussion

Charles Amos:

Which one piece of specific regulation would you get rid of in order to provoke the most innovation, in your view?

Matt Ridley:

Probably the precautionary principle, or rather, I would balance it with the innovation principle. I would tone it down, because I think it is genuinely causing real problems. So, for example, on genetically modified foods, we now know that we've missed out on significant improvements, not just in the economics of farming but in the ecology of farming, because they have reduced chemical use throughout the world. Yet, they're unavailable in Europe, and we've missed out on that, so that would be the one that I would go for.

Julio Alejandro:

I work with Liberland, Bitnation, a number of artificial intelligence, blockchain and 'intentional communities' like the Seasteading Institute. There have been a number of innovations within financial, commercial, ideas transactions and exchanges, but little has been done within centralised institutions such as governments, but also a physical place where individuals would be able to associate with each other. That's what we call an intentional community, also called a private city, or a charter city, a smart city. Would you think that that could be a new future of evolution, rather than from the digital side, but actually within the physical side of how to free people to interact with each other rather than creating digital transactions as with blockchain or artificial intelligence predictability?

Matt Ridley:

It's an interesting point. Paul Romer, of course, is the champion of the idea of a charter city, that somewhere in the world you should go to a poor country and say, 'Can we have a piece of your land and can we make a free-trade city in it and see if it works?'

I think it's a nice idea, but I don't think it's ever going to happen because, when push comes to shove, no country is going to hand over a chunk of their territory for this to happen. At one point, Paul had the idea that he could do this at Guantanamo

Bay, which sounded to me quite a good idea.

The founder of PayPal, Peter Thiel, makes the point that one of the reasons most innovation in the last ten years or so has been in the digital economy rather than the physical economy is because digital innovation is permissionless and physical stuff is not. We've essentially not got around to putting barriers in the way of innovation with bits. All our barriers are about innovation with atoms.

Of course, that's changing. Governments are starting to crack down on bits, as it were, quite fast at the moment, but I think that's an interesting point. We think of innovation, at the moment, as being very much a digital thing: artificial intelligence, blockchain, social media, all these kinds of things, and for the last generation, that's been true. But maybe that's because we've made it harder to innovate in the physical world. That's not to say there's been no innovation in the physical world. There has been quite a lot.

John Wilden Hughes:

Particularly for the young people present, can you just give, say, a couple of examples from your own really quite dense scientific experience—I know Cold Harbor and other places—where you actually think innovation can be quite smooth and can translate quite quickly? Just for encouragement.

Matt Ridley:

An example of an innovation that was or could be smoothly introduced. It depends what you mean by smoothly, but I used vaping and electronic cigarettes quite a lot in my talk as a case history, and it's a very interesting question as to why more people vape in the UK than in any other European country by about two and a half times, and why vaping is still banned in Australia but not here. Why vaping is catching up in America, but Britain is way ahead. It's got a diverse vaping industry. A lot more smokers have taken it up. Smoking rates are falling faster in the UK. In Japan, they've gone for a different technology, heat-not-burn cigarettes, and it's still pretty well illegal to take electronic cigarettes into Japan. I trace it back to a lucky accident, that early in the coalition government, David Halpern, head of the 'Nudge Unit', bumped into his old friend Rory Sutherland, the advertising executive, who was an early adopter of electronic cigarettes, and gave David Halpern a quick seminar on what these things were, and Halpern thought, 'That's interesting. These could actually help reduce smoking, rather than make the problem worse'.

He wrote a memo to David Cameron— everybody's called David in this story—the gist of which was 'when the public health experts come through the door and tell you to ban this thing, resist them, because this might be a good technology, not a bad technology'.

But then it got tangled up in the Tobacco Products Directive from the European Union, which banned advertising, and which slowed down the rate of smoking cessation in this country, etc. So, there have been hurdles, but that would be one example.

Another would be mitochondrial replacement therapy in the UK, again a superb piece of science dealing with a particularly rare disease. It came to parliament. We had a huge debate in both houses. Both houses passed it overwhelmingly. It went ahead. It then took a little longer to get going, because of various technical problems, but not because anyone was against it. So, it can be done.

Answer the questions

Male speaker:

How would you respond to genetic enhancement potentially limiting human freedom in the future?

Matt Ridley:

Limiting human freedom through genetic engineering, what's the risk of that? What's the prospect of that? Well, so far, reproductive and genetic technologies have been liberating. Think about the impact of in vitro fertilisation, test tube babies. It was thought this was going to be a tool for central-planning autocrats who

95

wanted to produce supermen. People were really, really worried in the 60s and 70s that, if in vitro fertilisation caught on and became easy to do, it would be used by people to basically make sure that everybody was the child of the supreme leader of the country, etc.

In fact, it had exactly the opposite effect. It enabled people who couldn't have children to have their own children. It liberated them. And the demand for Nobel Prize-winning sperm turned out to be extremely small, because people don't want Nobel Prize-winning fathers for their children, they want their own children. You know, they want children like them. So, I think the same will happen if we get anywhere close to designer baby-type technologies.

If you can go into a clinic in some years' time and be offered 46 genetic tweaks to your unborn child that will make it slightly more musical, slightly more intelligent, slightly better at sports or something, the 'slightly' is key. We now know that these factors come from huge numbers of genes, each with a very small effect, so you're probably going to have to choose about a thousand changes before you can make noticeable differences in these respects, and you don't know what the unintended consequences are. So, I just don't see it catching on.

But if you did it, I suspect the demand would be for people to get rid of problems, as it is now, with pre-implantation genetic screening. To get rid of disease risks, not to improve and enhance. So, I'm relatively relaxed about how people are going to use these technologies, certainly in terms of limiting human freedom.

Robert Cobbold:

I'm a huge fan of the idea that we need to remove

barriers to innovation, and I wonder if we need to take this insight all the way down into the realm of human consciousness, which evolves through a series of recognisable stages? One of the key insights of Integral Theory is that we've gone from a traditional stage of duty and those values, to a modernist stage of economic growth and secular values, to a postmodern stage. How can we take that insight into our own personalities? How can we remove barriers to innovation in our own evolution, as much as the evolution of technology?

Matt Ridley:

On the whole, I haven't really thought about that, I have to admit, and I think that the amount of cultural and economic and technological evolution we can do is now so overwhelmingly large and fast that I'm not too worried about changing our biology. We do, of course, change our biology. We've adapted to modern living. There's a fascinating book just coming out from Richard Wrangham about how we're a domesticated species. We've learned to gather in large groups and not attack each other, which chimpanzees can't do. This room would be chaos if we were chimpanzees. That's through a form of selection, of evolution.

I genuinely think that we have passed the buck to technological evolution, mostly, and that there's no point messing around by trying to encourage biological evolution in our species, because it's so slow and inadequate as a way of changing.

Jonathan Clark:

Shall we, then, abolish the British Academy and the Royal Society, prestigious bodies that have no other function than to be protectionist restraints on innovation?

99

Matt Ridley:

Well, since neither have elected me to their membership, I quite agree. [Laughter]

Lucy Neville-Rolfe:

I want you to be Chancellor for a moment, and tell us what you think about innovation incentives, things like R&D tax credits, given what you've said about the diffuse process of innovation.

Male speaker:

My question is actually similar. A couple of years ago, the government undertook a Patient Capital Review. My question is, how much do you think the inability to have patient investors restrains innovation?

Matt Ridley:

Well, I think my answers to Lucy's question and

the second question are probably fairly similar, inasmuch as I like anything that encourages research and development as long as it's not trying to pick winners and specifically singling ones out, and I worry about the catapults and things in that respect. Although they're not too bad there. But I do think that in this country we are chronically bad at the second stage, the patient capital, the build-up, the commercialisation. And we still think of innovation as invention-discovery, and actually, that's the 1 per cent inspiration that Edison talked about, not the 99 per cent perspiration.

Incentives to develop businesses out of these ideas are probably where the British focus needs to be to get over our inherent problems in that respect. So, I'm all for patient capital, and things like Entrepreneurs' Relief and EIS [Enterprise Investment Scheme] actually did have a big impact. The UK start-up ecosystem is actually pretty spectacular: since 2010, 600,000 start-ups a year, more than the rest of the European Union combined, much more than in the preceding ten years. Now, some of those are probably not very good, but Entrepreneurs' Relief and EIS have encouraged much more of that second-stage stuff, and we need to build on that and get it to keep working later.

Female speaker:

You suggested that you used hostility to innovation and the precautionary principle as a reason for voting leave, but my question is, given the current climate of Brexit negotiations, and particularly May's newly drafted deal, how plausible will it be for the UK to embrace innovation after leaving the EU?

Matt Ridley:

That brings me onto how to encourage

innovation outside the EU, if we are indeed outside the EU, and the high alignment that is apparently in the deal that we are about to hear about from the steps of Downing Street.

A high degree of alignment on goods in particular will make it very hard to do anything differently. Just to take gene editing, this technology that the rest of the world is saying doesn't need heavy and specific regulation and that the European Court has ruled does need heavy and specific regulation, and which, therefore, is bailing out of this country as fast as it can to Canada and other places. I'm talking about gene editing in agriculture. It'll be different when it comes to gene editing in medicine.

One of the things I was hoping we could do, if we left, was say, 'Right. Well, in that case, we'll recognise that it needs less regulation and can be fast-tracked into production'. It will be hard to embrace this aspect of Brexit with this deal, I can't deny that.

John Strafford:

Hayek wrote in *The Road to Serfdom* that when you have regulation upon regulation upon regulation, the end of the road is the totalitarian state, tyranny and dictatorship. I can see the end of the road in this country and in Europe. How can ordinary people use innovation to reverse that direction of travel?

Matt Ridley:

How do we use innovation to get around the drift towards a totalitarian state? Well, isn't it fascinating how we thought that the technologies that were coming along, starting with the fax machine and the mobile phone and going into the internet, were going to be incredibly liberating for the individual and were going to undermine the basis of state control of us?

Twenty years ago, we were so idealistic about this. It's almost hard to remember now, and the state has fought back and has found ways of using these technologies, whether it's through fake news or through surveillance, or whatever, to make us just as much under their thumb as before, perhaps more in some cases.

These things go in waves, though, and I do think that there will be opportunities to dissolve the power of totalitarians through technology, and on the whole the genie is out of the bottle. It would be relatively hard to set up an absolutely totalitarian state in a Western democracy, but it's proved surprisingly easy in some other countries in recent years, I have to say, and that's taken me by surprise.

Male Speaker:

I want to go back to something you spoke about earlier in your talk, about the FDA and about how potentially it has caused more harm than good through, essentially, picking winners, with a twenty-year process of getting approved. Obviously, it seems to me, the point of that is to prevent a snake oil salesman selling you a cabbage pill that he claims will cure your cancer. So, I want to ask, what do you think is the best way to balance an ex ante system of testing with an ex post system of specifically targeting fraudsters? Alternatively, do you think those kinds of fears are overblown?

Matt Ridley:

I don't feel I'm enough of an expert on the FDA and medical regulation to give you a very full answer here. Clearly, we don't want another

Thalidomide. We need to be testing things before they get put into human beings, etc. But we must, at the same time, encourage new ideas and new technologies to come forward. I don't feel we've got the balance right at the moment. If you look at what drug companies spend the monopoly profits they get out of patents on, it's not necessarily R&D. It's basically marketing, a lot of it, so it's reinforcing the monopoly as well. I think one needs to address that question. There are things like allowing orphan drugs to be tested in different conditions; allowing people who are dying to try drugs so that they can contribute knowledge about the safety of medicines, and so on; there are all sorts of imaginative ways that can be tried.

Robert Afia:

Competition, I would have thought, is a big

generator of innovation. So, encourage competition and would you not get more innovation?

Matt Ridley:

Competition, absolutely, but I sometimes think that free-market people talk about competition too much, and cooperation too little. Actually, what goes on vertically within a market is cooperation between the buyer and the seller, whereas the horizontal stuff between two sellers competing is very important, it's a crucial part of it, but I feel it puts people off if we talk about that too much and don't talk about the collaboration that can come from the way people work for each other in these sorts of worlds. Competing with yourself to deliver a better product to your customer is just as important as competing with someone else, I think.

第3章

创新、增长与
可能的未来

Innovation, growth and
possible futures

斯蒂芬·戴维斯
Stephen Davies

引言

在过去的几年里，人们已经意识到创新对现代世界的至关重要性。正是创新产生了这个世界的独特特征，持续的集约增长是其中的首要特征；创新还使我们的世界与我们祖先的世界截然不同。这就是迪尔德丽·姆茨克洛斯基巨著的三个部分的主旨，她在这部杰作中甚至主张我们应该停止使用"资本主义"一词，而只能谈论创新及其所需。我自己也提出了类似的观点，尽管在如何解释过去250年来创新的速度和强度突然增加的问题上，我与姆茨克洛斯基的看法略有不同（姆茨克洛斯基，2007，2010，2017；戴维斯，2019）。然而，强调创新是理解现代性的关键，正如马特·里德利的这场讲座所表明的那样，这种强调十分普遍。鉴于这一公认的事实，理解什么是创新，创新从何而来，为什么创新在历史上比过去200年少得多，以及如何阻碍甚至阻止创新，是一个非常重要的问题。

曾经有许多经济学理论试图解释经济增长现象，并找出自1750年左右以来世界经济增长的根本原因。这些理论涵盖了贸易和劳动分工的影响以及市场的范围（亚当·斯密）和政府，特别是国家政府在刺激发明方面的积极作用（许多作者）。然而，在过去20年左右的时间里，人们形成了一个共识，那就是得到正确答案的经济学家是熊彼特：经济学家们现在指出，创业、创新和创造性破坏的风暴才是真正创造财富和不断增长的源泉。

里德利特别关注创新的来源以及社会基础，即产生创新的那些社会关系，没有这些社会关系，创新就不可能发生。这就引出了以下内容，即当代世界的某些趋势是多么危险，应该予以谴责和抵制，因为它们对于为现代世界带来无与伦比的财富和舒适的那种持续创新来说，可能是致命的。在讲座中，

他就创新的社会性质和基础提出了一些值得重视和
拓展的观点。当人们提出并探讨这些观点时，就会
对当前世界经济的核心问题得出激进的、甚至令
人惊讶的结论。当把他的分析放在一个时间较长和
地域范围更广的历史视角中时，情况就更是如此。
与此同时，也有一些反对他这一立场的争议有待解
决，尽管我同意他关于历史最终会做出何种裁决的
判断，但至少在某个特定案例中，我们可以说陪审
团仍然没有定论。

马特·里德利在哈耶克讲座的主要论点

◁◁◁◁◁◁◁◁◁◁◁◁

马特·里德利在哈耶克讲座提出了几个论点。其中的核心论点是，马特·里德利认为创新不是英雄般的远见卓识者或罕见的杰出个人的产物，而是大量平凡、有求知欲、有进取心的人以及他们之间相互作用的产物。因此，这一论点反驳了艾茵·兰德在《源头》一书中表达的观点：进步和创新来自普罗米修斯式的人物，人类的其余成员最终会追随他们，并从他们的创造力中受益。相反，创新是一种社会现象，任何特定的创新都有许多根源和开创者，其中的大多数人都会被人们遗忘，甚至不为人所知。对于创新，重要的是贸易的社会框架以及商品和思想在人们之间的自由交换。里德利有力地指出，在与世界其他地区的贸易、交流和联系减少或缺失的地方，创新往往不会发生，实际上可能会发生倒退。这方面的经典例子是，在西罗马帝国瓦解和阿拉伯征服者造成地中海航道中断之后西欧的命运。正如布赖恩·沃德-珀金斯所指出的那样，其结果是贸易下降，财富和生产出现灾难性的减少，以及一系列技术的系统性丧失（罗马混凝土作为其中一项技术，也是刚刚才被重新发现①）（2006）。

由此引出了里德利的第二个论点，创新和创造力是人类自愿互动的产物。这意味着，试图通过蓄意的政治行动来规划或鼓励创新和创造力是徒劳的，甚至适得其反——特伦斯·基利（Terence Kealey，1996）已经非常有力地指出了这一点。这也意味着，限制人与人之间的互动和交流将阻碍甚至阻止创新。正如他指出的那样，创新过程中的困难，与其说是产生最初的想法或愿景（虽然这已经十分困难），不如说是将愿景转化为有益的、实用的

---

① 有关最近重新发现的罗马混凝土的秘密，请参阅犹他大学关于海水如何强化古罗马混凝土腐蚀海水促进稀有矿物的生长的研究内容。

创新，从而带来财富和人类福祉的增长。正是这样一个修补、试验和边际改进的过程，需要数百万人的自由互动，不仅需要思想的交流，还需要产品、商品和服务畅通无阻的交换。

在音乐和烹饪等领域，由此带来创新和创造力的方式是显而易见的。人与人之间的互动和贸易导致了新的烹饪和音乐形式的试验和发展。其中一个重要方面是文化混血儿的出现，他们结合了来自世界不同文化和地区的知识与见解。例如，大多数英国人所熟悉的印度料理实际上是莫格来（Mughlai）（即回族食物）烹饪，即莫卧儿人的菜肴，它将印度本土的技术和原料和来自莫卧儿人的中亚故乡的其他技术和原料（例如酸奶的使用），还有其他由阿拉伯商人和葡萄牙人带到印度的原料（例如土豆、西红柿和辣椒）结合起来。一个非常重要的结论是，认为全球贸易正在创造一个文化统一的世界是完全错误的——事实上，它创造了恰恰相反的更大的多样性和多元性，以及更大的创新（科文，2004）。

讲座的一个关键论点是，创新会导致经济增长和生产力的提高（从而带来更多的财富），因为它释放了时间这种最终稀缺的资源，使其可以被用于其他活动，从而带来更多的产出。在这里，我要对这个论点稍加限定。创新确实会提高时间的使用效率和强度，但创新对所有资源，包括各种原材料的作用同样如此。这一规则的一个可能的例外是能源，但从长远来看，即便如此也不是真的，我们将在后面看到这一点。这就是为什么过去三个世纪的长期趋势是原材料的实际成本下降，尽管这表明原材料已经被"用完了"，但实际上却更丰富。原因是使用集约度的提高，这意味着，例如，50年前需要1千克铜的产品现在只需要很少的铜，甚至不需要铜，铜可以被玻璃等替代品取代。一个重要的结论是，对于自动化破坏有偿工作的担忧是错误的，因为它已经持续了200多年。然而，正如我们将看到的那样，这并不意味着我们不该考虑与创新相关的其他担忧。

我对讲座的最后一个主要论点持有一定异议，这就是更大的历史视角实际上可以加强这个论点，使其更有根据，并使我们更清楚我们现在到底面临什么样的创新威胁。这一论点是，特定的创新在时机成熟之前是不可能发生的，因为许多其他创新必须先发生，之后的创新才有可能发生。此外，当这些早期的创新发生后，对其他创新的需要将变得前所未有的迫切，这就导致了对如何促成这些创新所进行的大量实验和探索。电话就是一个例子，在电气技术充分发展之前，电话是不可能出现的。在19世纪后期日益城市化和全球化的世界中，人们迫切需要一种有效的远距离语音交流手段，这意味着许多人正通过不断交流思想和技术寻找这种手段——亚历山大·格雷厄姆·贝尔只是其中之一。里德利甚至对任何时候可能出现的创新现象都不屑一顾，直到有人有了这种远见。他举出轮式行李箱通常被视为创新的例子，以此说明这种创新可能早在出现之前就已经出现了，但在某些其他创新出现之前，这种行李箱是不可能被创造出来的。

这一论点有许多深远的启示。第一，创新是不断累积的——这就是为什么创新的频率随着时间的推移而加快，而创新传播的时间却在缩短。第二，只要有足够的人员和畅通无阻的贸易与思想交流这一前提条件，创新的过程就是渐进和持续的。第三，同时也是主要的一组启示是历史性的。如果创新是解释现代（1750年后）世界持续发展和生活水平不断提高的原因，如果创新确实是一个长期累积过程的结果，在这个过程中，每一项创新都依赖于之前的创新，没有之前的创新就不会有后来的创新，这意味着，现代世界的持续集约增长不可能在实际发生之前发生。因此，用沃尔特·惠特曼·罗斯托（Walt Whitman Rustow）的话说，18世纪中叶之后的变化是一次腾飞，只有当创新、人口和世界不同地区之间的相互联系达到临界水平时，才有可能实现这一腾飞。最后，这意味着，只要产生创新的贸易和交流过程能够持续足够长的时间，现代世界在某种意义上就是不可避免的。

这一论点蕴含着很多道理。特别是，某些特定的创新显然依赖于其他更早或者实际上同步进行的创新。其中，实际上不可知的事情之一是，由于这些先决条件尚未得到满足，或者对这些先决条件的感知需求尚未变得明显，所以这些创新还没有发生，我们只能谈论已经发生的创新。然而，这种情况需要严格限定。比实际发生得更早的创新可能比里德利设想的要长。例如，集装箱船的出现确实需要在组织和管理方面先取得某些技术突破和创新，但这些先决条件在集装箱船实际出现之前几十年就已经满足了。换句话说，创新存在很大的滞后性。然而，这并不是需要作出的主要限定。

真正的问题是，有大量证据表明，我们称之为现代性的创新的加速和持续可能在它出现之前就已经开始了。如果我们审视人类历史的长河，会惊讶地发现，当人们考虑日常生活的模式和结构或绝大多数人的生活水平时，事情的变化是如此的微小。在一些反复出现的事件中，我们看到了创新的爆发和持续密集增长的初步迹象，通常是在地球的某个特定区域（《戈德斯通》，2002）。这些事件与其他三件事相关：地球上很大一部分地区存在稳定的政府、开放的知识探索和讨论，以及更高水平的贸易和交流，包括相对复杂的金融形式的出现。例如，在2世纪，地中海周围地区就发生过一次这样的事件，另外两次分别发生在8世纪末9世纪初的中东部分地区和12世纪的西欧部分地区。所有这些事件都有重大的创新和发现。然而，它们并没有持续下去，因为事情又回到了相对停滞的历史常态，在许多情况下，产生的技术和创新随后会被遗忘并遗失。

这类事件中最重大和最重要的事件发生在12世纪和13世纪的中国，即在非凡的宋代。宋朝有意鼓励贸易和商业，其结果是新思想和新技术的爆发，导致了18世纪之前全世界范围内最重要的经济增长。到了宋朝的后期，在13世纪，中国的技术发展和知识水平与西欧在18世纪初至中期达到的水平相同。这表明，如果创新活力继续保持下去，我们现在所谈论的无疑将是13世纪中国的"工业革命"，而不是18世纪英国的工业革命。假设在这种与事实相反的情况下，增长和创新自那时以来一直持续下去，我们可能会富裕得多（爱德华兹公司，2013）。那么，为什么没有发生这种情况呢？

创新的历史障碍

◁◁◁◁◁◁◁◁◁◁◁

　　我认为，问题的答案是我们不能相信的，在18世纪发生的在持续创新方面的突破，在某种程度上是不可避免的，或者是一个长期累积发现过程的结果。相反，正是在这种情况下，导致早期创新结束的力量和因素无法重复发挥作用。现实情况是：创新确实是普通人之间贸易和交流的自然和必然结果，但也有强大的力量与之对抗，限制了创新。从历史上看，直到最近这些力量都被证明是比较强大的。这些力量也是自然的，因为它们和创新一样，来自常见的人类互动。这里有两种力量或结构在发挥作用。

　　第一种力量是自发保险关系和社会制度，这是人类社会典型的产物。对我们几乎所有的祖先来说，压倒性的生活现实是，他们生活在一个马尔萨斯式的世界，一个物资极度匮乏的世界。在这个世界里，由于缺乏持续的创新，有时也由于人口少、人口密度低等结构性原因，很难提高资源的使用强度和效率。总的说来，从中长期来看，各类产出的增长速度与人口增长速度持平，甚至略低。偶尔会有意外的收获，但这些都是阶梯式的变化，而不是生产相对于人口持续上升的一部分。其结果是，生活水平没有提高，在历史的大部分时间里，绝大多数人生活在勉强糊口的边缘。一种几乎普遍的应对办法是，人们应制定制度、规则、规范和做法，以防范突发事件，特别是保护人们免受变化的影响，无论这种变化是自然变化还是人类行动的结果。其中包括分享种子或工具等关键资源或者土地轮休规则（就像中世纪欧洲敞田制），它还包括禁止在严格限制的市场之外购买商品以期在市场或其他地方以更高价格转售的做法，以及根据规范的"公正价格"（通常是传统价格）制定各种价格（包括工资）的规则。这样做的目的是保护人们免受意想不到的变化和偶然性的影响，同时也是为了防止人们比他们的同伴们做得明显更好（当然，这并没有阻止他们尝试——关键是这样做是不被认可的，而且难度很大）。然而，主要目的是让生活，特别是经济生活变得更可预测和稳定，并将变化的影响降至最低。

这些在几乎所有的前现代社会中都以不同的形式存在的制度和做法，现在通常被称为"道德经济学"，这个术语由历史学家爱德华·帕尔默·汤普森（1991）发明，人类学家詹姆斯·斯科特（1976）更广泛地应用。悲剧性的悖论是，虽然它们是对马尔萨斯式世界状况的一种回应，但它们阻碍或完全阻止了促使逃离马尔萨斯陷阱的那种持续创新。鉴于上述原因，这些规范、制度和做法的中心目标是将变化及其影响降至最低，因此这是一个不可避免的结果。重要的是，我们要认识到，道德经济的大多数制度与导致创新的交易和交换形式一样，都是社会互动的自发结果。这是因为这两种活动都反映了人类本性和动机的深层特征。亚当·斯密所说的

"易货和交换"的欲望，源于通过和平交换来改善自身状况的冲动，关键是尝试新事物的冲动。然而，许多人害怕改变，这在历史上往往有充分的理由。此外，即使可以客观地证明变革已经导致了条件的改善，但变革往往是一种经验，被视为一种损失而不是一种收获。因此，自发的人类互动不仅会导致创新，还会导致限制或阻止变化和创新的反应和行动，这是人类社会的另一个强大特征。

然而，这本身可能还不足以解释诸如在宋代的中国或阿巴斯时期中东地区激烈创新事件是如何逐渐消失的。这类事件带来了显著的利益，表现为更高的财富和收入，但它们也带来了颠覆性的变化（这与经济效益密切相关），这肯定会导致社会对创新的反应。尽管如此，我们应该注意到，道德经济的一些规则和制度（如禁止转售的法律，或控制交易准入的公会）涉及利用政治权力来执行这些法律。这就引出了历史上制约创新的第二个因素，即统治阶级和特权精英的作用。

在马尔萨斯式的物质匮乏的世界中，除了自发的社会保险（道德经济学）之外，相对于人口而言，针对生产这块"馅饼"的缓慢增长或零增长的情况，还存在第二种应对措施。这就是掠夺，不是通过贸易和交换，而是通过使用武力或欺诈手段从其他人那里获取资源。从历史上看，生产交换和掠夺是获取收入和资源的两种方式。这就是说，每个社会都有两大类社会阶级，一类是生产阶级或"勤劳"阶级（过去曾这样称呼他们），另一类是游手好闲的阶级或剥削阶级。后者控制着我们可以称之为掠夺的手段——致命的力量和系统性的混淆。换句话说，他们是统治阶级，他们最终不是靠生产和交换生活，而是靠从生产阶级那里榨取租金生活（丹克瓦特·亚历山大·鲁斯托，1980）。然而，纯粹或过度掠夺的统治阶级不会持续很长时间。更精明的统治阶级只榨取能让生产阶级继续生活和工作的东西，他们还提供了一系列所谓的公共产品，使和平贸易与生产变得更加容易（从而为自己创造更多、更稳定的租金）。最突出的是防止其他外部掠夺者和内部暴力与掠夺，以及和平解决争端的手段（外部防御和法律制度），但我们也可以包括稳定的货币和统一的度量衡，以及在他们控制的领土内进行自由交换。

从本质上讲，统治阶级对创新和由它所创造的经济增长有着复杂的看法。一方面，创新是受欢迎的：这为他们创造了更多可以征税的财富，并为他们创造了更多租金，可以用在修建宫殿、令人印象深刻的公共工程和享受奢华的生活上。然而，另一方面，这对他们也是一种威胁。他们处于现有社会等级的顶端，为什么要欢迎变革，特别是在他们地位不稳定的情况下？此外，创新及其给普通人和生产阶级成员带来更多的财富，这削弱了统治阶级对他们的控制，使他们拥有更大的自主权和行动自由。这就是为什么在历史上，统治集团往往通过法院或给予公会等机构法定特权等措施来执行其规范和规则，以支持道德经济的反创新机构，这意味着故意阻止技术、商业或金融方面的创新。这里还有另一个因素在起作用：那些在自愿生产和贸易领域取得成功，并因此获得财富的人，往往担心自己的财富会被雄心勃勃的年轻新贵抢走，因此他们求助于政治权力即统治阶级，以保护自己的地位，并巩固自己的地位，使其不受进一步变化的影响。在最极端的情况下，统治集团会故意和系统地阻止创新。

因此，尽管创新确实由普通人通过贸易和交流制度的互动产生，尽管许多创新确实需要在之前进行过其他创新才能成为可能（因此赋予创新过程累积性），但这并不意味着我们称之为现代性的创新爆发是不可避免的，而且不可能比它更早发生。证据表明，尽管几乎可以肯定的是，在现代创新发生之前，特定的因素必须到位或达到临界水平，但这些条件早在18世纪之前就已经满足了。此外，关键的问题是，为什么18世纪始于欧洲西北部的创新热潮并没有像早期那样消退，而是持续不断，并且确实加速了。在这种情况下，创新的力量能够战胜在早期扼杀持续创新的社会体制和统治阶级。为什么会这样呢？

欧洲腾飞的解读

◁◁◁◁◁◁◁◁◁◁◁◁

如果里德利关于创新和创新过程的论述是正确的，那么这一论述本身就给我们提供了关于这个问题的答案可能是什么的想法。从广义上讲，基于贸易和交换的社会互动和关系，比基于权力和对变化表现出恐惧的社会机制的社会互动和关系变得更为强大和广泛。社会从恐惧新事物变成了追求新事物。

有三种具体的变化。首先，一些统治阶级（或者更准确地说，是一些足以有所作为的统治阶级成员）开始支持创新，并利用政治权力扫除社会和法律障碍来帮助创新（乔尔·莫基尔，2011，2018）。其次，出现了一些社会利益联盟，它们意识到自己从创新和自愿行动中获得了利益。大约在

1770—1860年，它们与一个反对创新及创新带来的变化的利益联盟经常发生激烈的政治和社会或文化冲突——第二个群体既包括一些精英，也包括下层阶级的成员，特别是农民和传统手工业者。在大多数情况下，支持创新的力量取得了胜利（尽管他们在导致创新的原因以及如何在控制创新的同时鼓励创新的问题上存在分歧）。最后，出现了文化转变，创新和企业开始受到赞赏和效仿，而不是使人害怕和受人贬低（麦克洛斯基，2007，2010，2017）。有几种理论可以解释为什么这三种力量在当时当地变得强大到足以克服反作用力，但由于篇幅有限，这里不做赘述。

然而，这远远没有结束这场争论。首先，它提出了一个大问题，即里德利所认为的创新过程是否像他认为的那样有益——有许多人不同意他的观点。更严重的是，我们必须问一问这一次是否真的不同。我们在过去200年左右的时间里所看到的持续且不断加速的创新是否会继续下去，发展到所谓的奇点，之后情况将迅速变得如此不同，以至于我们甚至无法想象或描述它们将是什么样子？或者，是否有理由认为，对创新的重视是夸大其词，我们只是生活在迄今为止最长、最戏剧性的一段创新时期，它将像所有其他时期一样结束并消失？也许最紧迫的是，我们会不会意外和无意地重现在人类历史上大部分时间里都适用的条件和激励措施，从而使创新就此结束？

反对创新的论点

◁◁◁◁◁◁◁◁◁◁◁

在某些方面，第一个问题实际上是最容易回答的。自现代化开始以来，就有人谴责创新，特别是技术创新。一个共同的主题是关注创造性破坏带来的代价（破坏部分，例如因创新而消失的生计和职业），而忽视创造性部分（这些创新带来的新的、不同的产品、职业和生活方式）。更深刻的论点是，持续创新的过程及其所创造的世界本身就存在问题。这一立场——包括约翰·拉斯金和威廉·莫里斯在内的一系列作者，以及约翰·泽赞和"大学航空炸弹客"泰德·卡辛斯基（2016，2018）等当代原始主义者和深层生态主义者已经阐明激进批评家的立场是，持续的创新在某种意义上是不虔诚的，因为它破坏了自然秩序，创造了一种与我们作为生物的本性背道而驰的生活方式。结论是，如果不加以制止并扭转，就会产生灾难性的生态和社会后果。

对这类论点的回应是直截了当的：它在经验上是错误的。正如里德利和朱利安·林肯·西蒙等作者所表明的那样，技术创新的效果一直是，并将继续减少人类对环境的影响。其模式是通过创新来加强旧的处事方式，并将其推到一定的限度和规模，在这个极限和规模上，它确实开始产生不利影响。然而，在这一点上，里德利所描述的修补和基于交换的过程导致了问题解决方式的进一步创新。目前的一个例子是农业，特别是畜牧业，它对生物圈产生了负面影响，但由于养殖肉类的发展等创新，畜牧业看起来几乎将被完全取代。就人类的福祉而言，显而易见的反驳是，在大多数情况下，厌恶技术者和新勒德主义者对放弃自己生活中的创新成果没有任何热情（除了一些值得尊敬的人之外）。无论在什么地方，绝大多数人都会选择接受创新及其结果，而不是他们祖先的生活。

创新和增长是否可持续？

◁◁◁◁◁◁◁◁◁◁◁

另一种不同的论点是，创新带来了巨大的利益，但创新和我们生活的世界是不可持续的，也不会继续下去。一般情况是，由于世界的物理限制，创新和增长不可能无限期地持续下去。虽然在极端情况下是正确的，但这方面的大多数论点再次遭到事实的驳斥。此外，正如里德利在讲座中指出的那样，创新的关键资源是知识和想法，而且它们的结合和重组方式是人类互动的结果。就我们而言，这是一个庞大到近乎无限的资源。更严肃的论点涉及一种特别的资源，即能源，或者更准确地说，是可用的能源，尤其是化石燃料。

该论点是指，我们在现代世界看到的增长不是创新的结果，而是因为人类利用了化石燃料中积累的能源。从这个角度看，我们现在的创新水平更高，这是经济增长的结果，而不是原因。进一步的论点是，过去存在大量的创新，但这些创新没有带来增长——缺少的成分是能源。这种观点的问题并不在于我们会在物理层面耗尽化石燃料或能源。相反，我们面临的挑战是，随着时间的推移，获取石油（尤其是从地面开采石油）所需的能源量不断增加，这可以通过EROEI（能源投资回报）比率来衡量。在20世纪早期，从地下开采近100桶石油需要相当于1桶石油的能量，但现在这一比例约为20∶1，而且还在下降。人们普遍认为，我们可以简单地用其他可再生能源取代化石燃料，但这种说法遭到了驳斥，理由有两个。首先，可再生能源的能源投资回报率太低，无法支撑复杂的工业文明（例如，生产风力涡轮机和太阳能电池板等产品的能源成本），而且从理论上讲，这一点不会改变是有原因的。其次，有一些事情可以用石油来完成，但不能用任何可再生能源来完成，因为可再生能源太分散，很难储存——相比之下，石油非常轻巧且紧凑，而且包含了大量可用能量。

如果这是真的，那么无论有多少创新，现代的增长都将慢慢结束，我们将恢复到历史常态（在大约70到200年的时间里——大多数持这种观点的作者认为这个过程已经开始）（格里尔，2017，2019）。随着增长下滑，贸易和交换也随之下滑，创新也会随之下滑并回到历史常态。这一论点值得认真对待，鉴于目前的技术，它对可再生能源的批评是尖锐而有效的。但问题是，我们实际上可以看到，解决这一挑战所需要的是一种什么样的创新：一种储存、运输和最重要的压缩可用能源的方法，无论能源来自何方（如果你愿意，可以使用超级电池）。如果马特·里德利提出的创新过程模型是正确的，那么除非其他方面发生变化，否则我们应该会看到这一创新的实现会按照他所描述的方式发生，通过大量人的互动所带来的许多零星变化（正如他所说，我们已经看到电池技术的重大发展）。当然，这也有

136

可能不会发生，也许是因为必要的创新和发现不会及时发生。在这种情况下，我们的未来无疑是黯淡的。然而，只要其他因素阻碍创新进程的方式不发生改变，创新就有可能发生。

创新的速度是否已经放缓？

◁◁◁◁◁◁◁◁◁◁◁

　　一些经济学家和其他人提出的另一种观点是，创新实际上在一段时间前就达到了顶峰，这是有结构性原因的。这一论点由乔纳森·许布纳于2005年提出，其他学者，特别是泰勒·科文、西奥多·莫迪斯和罗伯特·詹姆斯·戈登对其进行了阐述（科文，2011；莫迪斯，2002；戈登，2000）。这里的论点是，在过去的三四十年里，以一些指数衡量的创新速度已经显著放缓。这被认为是发达经济体自20世纪70年代以来增长率明确下降的原因。根据这一观点，创新的高峰或至少是导致生产力发生重大变化的创新出现在19世纪后期和20世纪初期。这种观点认为，从那时起，我们基本上一直在填补空白，完善那些早期的根本性突破。这方面的研究，特别是莫迪斯的研究，大部分都是针对汉斯·莫拉维克（1990）和雷蒙德·库茨魏尔（2006）等作者的论点，即我们实际上看到的是正在加速的创新，这将使我们在不久的将来迎来技术奇点（如前所述）。怀疑论者的论点是，与大多数过程一样，创新是自我限制的，通常遵循S形曲线。最初，发明和创新的速度不断加快，随后，创新的步伐逐渐放慢，最终趋于平稳。对此最常见的解释可引用马特·里德利在他的讲座中讨论的一个现象。创新会导致专业化水平的提高（比如说，随着时间得到释放，我们不再需要80%的劳动人口从事农业生产）以及劳动分工不断细化。换句话说，创新导致了社会复杂程度的提高。这种观点的问题是，这种更大的复杂性最终会使有效的创新变得更加困难，因为它提高了建立个人和知识之间至关重要的联系的成本。在这种情况下，创新确实是一个最终自我限制的过程，或者至少是一个长期停滞的过程。

　　创新的速度是否真的放缓了其实是一个很难解

答的问题，因为很多争论都是定性的，而不是纯粹定量的。争论的焦点不仅仅是专利数量减少了，还包括我们现在取得的创新相对而言都是微不足道的，并不像电力和内燃机等早期创新那样改变了我们的生活或提高了生产力。对此，存在两种反应。第一种是，现在判断许多较新的创新是否会像早期的创新那样产生巨大的影响还为时过早。马特·里德利在讲座中提出的一个主要观点恰恰与此相关：我们倾向于系统地高估创新在短期内的影响，而低估其长期影响。这种论点在戴维·埃哲顿（2019）的著作，尤其是他的《旧事物的震撼：1900年以来的科技与全球历史》一书中得到了支持。乍一看，这似乎与里德利提出的情况相反，因为他认为，在技术的历史上，新奇性被夸大了，而我们却忽视了旧有技术与工艺的持久力，甚至在某些情况下，忽视了以前被抛弃的技术的复兴。正如他所说，流行杂志中充斥着本来要发生并改变世界但并未发生和改变世界的技术和创新，而非常古老的技术却在人们不注意的情况下继续存在。不过，他所描绘的图景与里德利的观点非常相似。

创新并不是英雄发明家或重大变革性突破的产物，而是个人修补和试错带来零星变化的过程——大规模研发的作用被高估了——而所有这些个别的微小变化和边际改进的累积效应才具有变革性。大多数创新的失败，往往是因为虽然在技术上可行，但经济成本太高，或者因为它们试图将不相容的功能结合起来（超音速客运是前者的例子之一，飞行汽车是后者的例子之一）。这意味着，现代世界的创新过程既快又慢：快是因为想法和实验的数量越来越多，频率越来越高；慢是因为微小的变化需要时间才能累积成质变的东西。

对所谓的创新放缓的另一种反应是，这种情况是真实存在的，但不是由内在因素造成的，如创新产生的更大复杂性的反馈效应，而是因为政治和社会变化。这个论点很有说服力，与里德利讲座中的一个主要观点直接相关，也可能是当今现代性创新进程所面临的最大威胁。

创新和增长面临的主要威胁

◁◁◁◁◁◁◁◁◁◁◁◁

　　鉴于里德利对于创新的社会基础，以及最终的集约化增长和现代世界的看法，阻碍这一进程甚至阻止这一进程的想法和信念、公共政策或法律，都可能产生（可能是意料之外的）阻止创新的结果。如果像我所说的那样，现代性的持续创新并不是某些因素达到临界水平的必然结果，而只是因为克服了以前阻止这种腾飞的其他结构性力量，那么，我们完全有可能有意或无意地使历史回归常态。过去两个半世纪的持续创新和增长，实际上只是漫长历史的又一段插曲。

　　有三种动力可能会造成这种情况。首先，理论上旨在鼓励创新的法律和制度的影响，但考虑到这

里提出的对于创新的理解，这些法律和制度实际上
会扼杀创新。里德利所举的主要例子就是知识产
权。从理论上讲，专利和版权应该是通过授予发明
者一个有时间限制的垄断权来鼓励有风险的创新，
这将产生垄断租金（超常收入）。说得委婉一些，
这有许多问题。除了产权是对资源稀缺及其引发的
冲突的回应这一哲学问题外，尽管信息是一种丰富
的非稀缺性资源，这一问题还有一些实际困难。主
要的实证问题是，没有明确的证据表明，从历史上
看专利鼓励了生产性创新。里德利提出的理论实际
上导致了相反的结论，即专利阻碍了创新。如果说
创新是思想交流的产物，是有进取心的个人努力改
进或改造别人在他们之前所做的东西的产物，那么
任何使这一过程的成本变得更高、时间更长，或者
在极端的情况下完全阻止这一过程的行为，都会阻
碍创新。就目前而言，有充分的证据表明，特别是
美国所倡导和执行的那种知识产权制度，通过对现
有技术的复制和改进，阻碍了创新。它还为专利巨
头提供了大量的寻租机会，这些专利巨头仅仅将专

利作为通过无理取闹的诉讼来增加收入的手段，并创造了一个知识产权租借者阶层，他们不是通过创新，而是通过国家赋予他们的垄断权来获得财富和收入。此外，知识产权通过限制所有者以各种侵入性方式使用实物商品，日益损害了实际实物商品的不动产权，这也阻碍了创新。

　　第二个问题是态度、思想和信仰及它们在现代民主社会中产生的政治问题。这里的挑战是指对创新及其带来的变化持续存在恐惧和不安，这导致了来自两个方面的压力，要求采取措施减缓或停止特定创新，即使是一般的创新。第一种压力来自那些确实已经从特定创新的影响中失败的人，或者认为自己已经失败但实际上并非如此的人。第二种压力来自那些从以前的创新或现状中获得利益的人，他们担心持续的创新会损害自己的地位。这两种压力加在一起，一种是来自受威胁的精英阶层，另一种是来自更广泛的民众运动，可以产生一种非常强大的政治主张，刻意试图减缓变革或完全阻止变革。例如，我们可以从对优步（Uber）等"共享经济"

应用的抵制中看到这一点。当代许多政治主张，例如，抵制移民或支持保护主义，最终都反映了对创新与变革的恐惧，以及对变革成本与失败者而非收益与成功者的关注。此外，还有一些非常有影响力的想法也反映了这种观点。其中最有力的一种观点，也是里德利所讨论的，就是预防原则，即在我们确定一项创新不会产生有害影响之前，我们不应该进行创新。因为我们永远无法确定这一点，所以在实践中，如果认真对待的话，就会呼吁不要进行任何形式的改变或创新。此外，由于在许多情况下，什么都不做或不创新本身就是有风险的，所以这种论点是前后矛盾的，不能提供真正的行动指南。然而，就其影响政治辩论的程度而言，它可能产生非常有害的影响。与此相反的观点是"先行原则"，即我们应该尽早发现问题和挑战，以便在创新过程能够更快地产生解决问题的办法。

然而，最大的问题是第三个问题。知识产权和政治等机构因对创新的错误恐惧所引发的不良行为可能会造成损害，但它们现在无法阻止创新进程，除非它们在全球范围内运作。如果它们不这样做，这一进程将在世界上那些受其影响较小的地区继续下去。因此，尽管地球上可能有部分地区停滞不前，但作为一个整体，世界不会停滞不前。此外，世界上那些确实走上遏制创新之路的地区，将在许多方面落后于那些没有走上这条路的地区，最终这将变得令人无法忍受。然而，有一种事态发展可能在全球范围内对创新形成制约。这就是欧盟等超国家监管体制的发展，以及由所谓的贸易协定创建的全球协调监管网络。尽管此类协定的目的是通过消除所谓的非关税壁垒（实质上是相互冲突的监管制度，阻止了产品跨监管边界进行自由交易）来促进贸易和交换，但它们是通过协调监管制度来实现的。这创造了一种日益全球化和标准化的监管模式。

这对创新进程来说非常危险，因为它有可能使前文所述的统治者面临的激励措施死灰复燃，但这一次是在全球范围内。一些统治阶级最终支持创新而不是试图遏制创新的一个主要原因是，他们面临着与控制地球上其他地区的其他精英竞争的现实。

他们只能在他们自己控制的地理区域执行法规，如果在高层次上执行，就会在竞争中处于不利地位。

此外，在近代历史的大部分时间里（直到20世纪30年代甚至20世纪50年代），监管的内容相当宽松和笼统，而不够具体和详细。现在，监管的范围巨大，体量庞大，而且非常详细和精确。这在一系列领域（制药只是其中最明显的例子）的作用是限制创新过程，并给推动创新的各种贸易和交换设置壁垒。

然而，试图通过消除监管冲突以及监管制度之间的竞争来解决这一问题，将会落入我们所说的帝国陷阱。统一世界大部分地区的帝国，创造了一个稳定的政府和交流的广泛领域。最初，这创造了更多的贸易和经济活力。然而，帝国统治者控制和遏制创新的动机极其强大，他们不再像较小国家的统治者那样害怕来自其他精英的竞争。目前的趋势是创建一个类似于全球监管秩序的体系，一个事实上的世界帝国。这肯定会阻止创新的进程，并恢复在有史以来大部分时间里引导大众进程和精英行动遏制创新的激励和条件。

马特·里德利清楚地解释了什么是创新，创新源于什么，以及创新带来的好处。他还列举了我们现在面临的一些危险，包括政治、文化和体制方面的危险。然而，我担心他仍然过于乐观。他认为现代创新世界是自然或不可避免的，是因为他没有意识到它的偶然性有多大，以及它的出现在多大程度上是偶然事件的结果。我们不应该认为创新是理所当然的，我们应该始终意识到，经常有一些出于善意的举动所带来的危机，以及错误想法和情绪的影响，将使创新停滞不前，并恢复到我们祖先的世界。

Introduction

In the last few years there has been a realisation of how central innovation is to the modern world. It is innovation that produces its distinctive features, above all sustained intensive growth, and makes our world so radically different from that of our ancestors. This is the main theme for example of Deirdre McCloskey's magnum opus in (so far) three parts, which goes so far as to argue that we should stop using the term 'capitalism' and simply speak of innovation and what it requires. I have also made a similar point myself, although I disagree slightly with McCloskey over how to explain the sudden increase in the pace and intensity of innovation in the last two hundred and fifty years (McCloskey 2007, 2010, 2017; Davies 2019). The emphasis on innovation as the key to understanding modernity is, however, widespread, as this lecture by Matt Ridley shows. Given that recognised fact, understanding what innovation is, where it comes from, why it has been much less common historically than in the last two hundred years, and how it can be hindered or even stopped, is a matter of great importance.

At one time there were many economic theories that tried to explain the phenomenon of economic growth and identify a fundamental cause for the kind of growth the world has seen since around 1750. These ranged from the impact of trade and the division of labour together with the extent of the market (Adam Smith) to the active role of governments, and national governments in particular, in stimulating invention (many authors). However, over the last two decades or so a consensus has emerged that the economist who got the correct answer was

150

Schumpeter: it is entrepreneurship, innovation and the gale of creative destruction that economists now point to as the source of genuine wealth-creating and increasing growth.

Ridley's lecture fits into the continuing discussion and addresses the questions set out earlier. In particular, he is concerned with the sources of innovation and with its social basis, the kinds of social relations that create innovation and without which it cannot happen. This leads to the point of how certain trends in the contemporary world are dangerous and should be deprecated and resisted because they are potentially fatal for the kind of sustained innovation that has brought about the unparalleled wealth and comfort of the modern world. In his lecture he makes a number of points that bear emphasis and expansion about the social nature and basis of innovation. When drawn out and explored these lead to radical and perhaps surprising conclusions about central aspects of the current world economy.

微妙的创新

This becomes even more the case when his analysis is placed into a chronologically longer and geographically wider historical perspective. At the same time there are arguments against his position that need to be addressed, and in at least one case we can say that the jury is still out, even though I share his judgement as to what the verdict of history will finally be.

The Hayek Lecture's main arguments

The Hayek Lecture sets out several arguments. The central one is that innovation is the product not of heroic visionaries or outstanding and rare individuals, but of large numbers of ordinary, enquiring and enterprising people and the interactions between them. Thus, it rejects the idea Ayn Rand expressed in *The Fountainhead*: that progress and innovation come from Promethean individuals, with the rest of humanity eventually following them and benefitting from their creativity. Instead, innovation is a social phenomenon, with any particular innovation having many parents and originators, most of them forgotten or even unknown.

What matters is the social framework of trade and the free exchange of both goods and ideas among people. Ridley powerfully makes the point that where trade, exchange and contact with the rest of the world are reduced or absent, innovation tends not to happen and regression can actually take place. The classic historical example of this is the fate of Western Europe in the aftermath of the collapse of the West Roman Empire and the disruption of Mediterranean sea routes by the Arab conquests. As Bryan Ward-Perkins (2006) has shown, the result was a decline in trade, a disastrous reduction in wealth and production and the systematic loss of a whole range of technologies (one of which, Roman concrete, has only just been rediscovered[①]).

Ridley's second argument, which follows from this, is that innovation and creativity are the product of voluntary human interaction. This means that it is

---

① For the recent rediscovery of the secret of Roman concrete, see https://unews.utah.edu/roman-concrete/.

futile and even counterproductive to try and plan it or encourage it by deliberate political action—a point Terence Kealey (1996) has made very powerfully. It also means that restraining human interaction and exchange will hamper or even prevent innovation. As he points out, the difficult thing in the process of innovation is not so much the generation of the original idea or vision (though that is difficult enough) but the conversion of the vision into a useful and practical innovation that brings about an increase in wealth and human well-being. It is that process of tinkering, experimentation and marginal improvement that requires the free interaction of millions of people and the unhindered exchange of not just ideas, but products, goods and services.

The way in which this brings about innovation and creativity can be seen very clearly in fields such as music and cuisine. Here, interaction and trade between people lead to experimentation and the development of new kinds of cuisine and forms of music. An important aspect of this is the appearance of cultural hybrids that combine knowledge and insight from different cultures and parts of the world. For example, the Indian cuisine that most British people are familiar with is actually Mughlai cooking, the cuisine of the Mughals, which combined indigenous Indian techniques and ingredients with others drawn from the Mughals' original homeland of Central Asia (the use of yoghurt for example) and yet others brought to India by Arab traders and the Portuguese (such as the potato, the tomato and the chilli pepper). One very important conclusion to draw is that it is completely wrong to believe that global trade is producing a world of cultural uniformity—in fact it creates the exact opposite, more diversity and variety, along with greater innovation (Cowen 2004).

A key argument of the lecture is that innovation leads to economic growth and increased productivity (and hence greater wealth) because it frees up time, the ultimate scarce resource, to be used for other activity and hence more output. Here I would qualify the argument slightly. Innovation does indeed lead to greater efficiency and intensity in the use of time but it does the same for all resources, including raw materials of all kinds. The one possible exception to that rule is energy, but even that is not true in the long run, as we shall see later. This is why the long-run trend over the last three centuries has been for the real cost of raw materials to decline, indicating that they are actually more abundant despite being 'used up'. The reason is the greater intensity of use, which means for example that a product that required a kilo of copper fifty years ago will now only require a fraction of that or even none, with the copper now replaced by a substitute such as glass. One important conclusion is that concern about automation destroying paid work is misplaced, as it has been for over two hundred years. However, this does not mean that other concerns about innovation should not be considered, as we shall see.

The final main argument of the lecture is the one

that I have some disagreement with and this is the point where greater historical perspective can actually strengthen the argument and make it better founded, as well as making it clearer exactly what kinds of threats to innovation we now face. The argument is that particular innovations cannot happen until the time is ripe, in the sense that a number of other innovations have to take place first before the later one becomes possible. Moreover, when those earlier innovations have happened the need for other innovations then becomes acute in a way that it was not before and this leads to lots of experimentation and exploration of how to produce them. An example would be the telephone, which was not possible until electrical technology had become sufficiently developed. Once it was, the acute need for an effective means of long-distance spoken communication in the increasingly urbanised and globalised world of the later nineteenth century meant that many people were working on a means of doing this with a constant

158

exchange of ideas and techniques—Alexander Graham Bell was only one of many. Ridley goes so far as to discount the phenomenon of innovations that could have occurred at any time until someone had the vision, arguing that the wheeled suitcase, often given as an example of an innovation that could have happened long before it did, could not have been introduced until certain other innovations had happened.

This argument has a number of far-reaching implications. The first is that innovation is cumulative— this is one reason why the frequency of innovations has accelerated over time and the time for the diffusion of innovations has shrunk. The second is that the process of innovation is gradual and continuous, as long as the preconditions of enough people and sufficient unhindered trade and exchange of ideas are in place. The third and major set of implications is historical. If innovation is what explains the modern (post-1750) world with its sustained growth and rising living standards, and if innovation is indeed the result of a long-run cumulative process in which each innovation rests on ones previously made, without which they could not come about, then several things follow. It means that the modern world of sustained intensive growth could not have happened before it actually did. The change after the middle of the eighteenth century was therefore a take-off (to use Walt Rustow's expression) that became possible only once a critical level of innovation, population and interconnections between different parts of the world had been reached. Finally, this means that the modern world was in some sense inevitable so long as the processes of trade and exchange that produce innovation had been allowed to continue for long enough.

There is a lot of truth in this model. In particular it is clearly true that certain specific innovations depend upon other ones being made earlier—or indeed at the same time. One of the things that is literally unknowable is the list of innovations that have not happened because those preconditions have not yet been met or the perceived need for them has not yet become manifest. We can only talk about the ones that have happened. However, this picture needs to be severely qualified. The list of innovations that could have happened earlier than they did may be longer than Ridley supposes. It is true for example that the container ship required certain prior technological breakthroughs and innovations in organisation and management, but those preconditions were met several decades before the container ship was actually introduced. There are significant lags in other words. However, that is not the main qualification that needs to be made.

The real problem is that there is much evidence to hand that the speeding up and sustaining of innovation that we call modernity could have started some time before it did. If we look at the long course of human history, what is striking is how little things change when one considers, for example, the patterns and structures of everyday life or the standards of living of the great majority of people. However, there are repeated episodes in which we see bursts of innovation and the first signs of sustained intensive growth, typically in a specific part of the planet (Goldstone 2002). These episodes correlate with three other things: stable government over a large part of the planet's surface, open intellectual enquiry and discussion, and a higher level of trade and exchange, including the appearance of relatively sophisticated forms of finance. There was one such episode in the lands around the Mediterranean in the second century, for example, another in parts of the Middle East in the later eighth and early ninth century, another in parts of Western Europe in the twelfth century. All of these episodes saw major innovations and discoveries. They did not last, however, as things reverted to the historical norm of relative stasis and in many cases the technologies and innovations that were produced were subsequently forgotten and lost.

The biggest and most significant episode of this kind took place in China during the twelfth and thirteenth centuries, under the remarkable Song dynasty. The Song, unlike previous and subsequent dynasties, deliberately encouraged trade and commerce and relaxed the extensive controls on the Chinese population that were a traditional part of China's imperial governance. The result was an outburst of new ideas and technologies, leading to the most significant episode of growth anywhere in the world before the eighteenth century. By the later years of the dynasty, in the thirteenth century, China had a level of technical development and knowledge that was the same as that reached by Western Europe in the early to mid eighteenth century. What this demonstrates is that had the episode of innovative dynamism continued, we would now no doubt be speaking of an industrial revolution of the thirteenth century in China rather than a British one in the eighteenth century. (We would also be far wealthier, assuming that in this counterfactual, growth and innovation had continued since then (Edwards 2013).) So why did this not happen?

Historical barriers to innovation

The answer, I believe, is one that means we cannot believe that the breakthrough into sustained innovation that did happen in the eighteenth century was somehow inevitable, or the conclusion to a long process of cumulative discovery. Rather it is the one case where the forces and factors that had brought earlier episodes to an end were unable to do so again. The reality is this: innovation is indeed the natural and inevitable result of trade and exchange among ordinary people, but there are powerful forces that work against that and limit innovation. Historically, these have proved stronger until recently. These forces are also natural in the sense that like innovation they arise from commonly found human interactions. There are two kinds of force or structure at play here.

The first are what we may call the spontaneous insurance relations and social institutions that human societies have typically produced. The overwhelming reality of life for almost all of our ancestors was that they lived in a Malthusian world, a world of severe scarcity. In this world, because of the lack of sustained innovation and sometimes for other, structural reasons such as low population and low population density, it was very difficult to increase the intensity and efficiency with which resources were used. Generally speaking, over the medium to longer term, output of all kinds grew at the same rate as or even slightly slower than human population. There were occasional windfall gains but these were step changes, not part of a continuous upward slope of production relative to population. The result was that living standards did not rise and for most of history the overwhelming majority lived at the edge of subsistence. One almost universal response was for people to develop institutions, rules, norms and practices that provided security against contingencies and in particular protected people against the effects of change, whether natural or the result of human action. These included things like rules for the sharing of access to key resources such as seeds or tools or the rotation of access to land (as in the medieval European open field system). It also included prohibitions on practices such as buying goods outside strictly limited markets with a view to reselling them at a higher price in the market or elsewhere, and rules that set prices of all kinds (including wages) according to a normative 'just price' which was typically the traditional one. The intention was to protect people against unexpected change and chance and also to prevent people from doing significantly better than their fellows (this didn't stop them trying of course — the point is that doing so was disapproved of and made difficult). The main aim, however, was to make life, and particularly economic life, more predictable and stable and to minimise the effects of change.

These institutions and practices, which were found in varying forms in almost all pre-modern societies, are now commonly referred to as the 'moral economy', a term invented by the historian E. P. Thompson (1991) and applied more widely by the anthropologist James Scott (1976). The tragic paradox is that while they were a response to the conditions of the Malthusian world, they hindered or outright prevented the kind of sustained innovation that leads to escape from the Malthusian cage. This was an inevitable result, given that, as said above, the central aim of these norms, institutions and practices was to minimise change and its effects. It is important to realise that most of the institutions of the moral economy were as much the spontaneous outcome of social interaction as the kind of trades and exchange that led to innovation. This was because both kinds of activity reflected deep-seated features of human nature and motivation. The desire to 'truck, barter and exchange' as Adam Smith put it, derives from the impulse to improve one's condition by peaceful exchange and, crucially, to try something new. However, many human beings are fearful of change, often historically for good reason. Moreover, change, even if it can be objectively shown to have led to improved conditions, is often experienced and perceived as a loss rather than a gain. So spontaneous human interaction does not only lead to innovation, it also leads to responses and actions that work to limit or prevent change and innovation, and this is another powerful feature of human societies.

However, that by itself is probably not enough to explain the way that episodes of intense innovation such as Song China or the Abbasid Middle East came to peter out. Episodes of that kind brought significant benefits in the shape of higher wealth and incomes, but they also brought disruptive change (which was intimately connected to the economic benefits) and this certainly led to a social reaction against the innovations. Nevertheless, we should notice that some of the moral economy's rules and institutions (such as laws against reselling, or guilds that controlled access to trades) involved the use of political power to enforce them. This brings us to the second factor that historically checked innovation, the role of ruling classes and privileged elites.

In the world of Malthusian scarcity there was a second response to the situation of slow to non-existent growth of the 'pie' of production relative to population besides spontaneous social insurance (moral economy). This was predation, acquiring resources from other people not by trade and exchange but through the use of force or fraud. Historically production and exchange on the one hand and predation on the other are the two ways of acquiring income and resources. This means that in every society there are two broad sets of social classes, the productive or 'industrious' classes (as they were once called), and the idle or exploitative classes. The latter control what we may call the means of predation—deadly force and systematic obfuscation. In other words, they are the ruling classes, who ultimately live off not production and exchange but rents extracted from the productive classes (Rustow 1980). (They often do own productive assets, particularly land, but this is a consequence of their controlling deadly force, not a cause as Marx thought). Ruling classes that are purely or excessively predatory do not last long, however. The more astute only extract as much as will allow the productive classes to continue to live and work. They also provide a range of so-called public goods that make peaceful trade and production easier (and so create larger and more stable rents for themselves). The most prominent are protection against other outside predators and against internal violence and predation, together with a means of settling disputes peacefully (so external defence and a legal system), but we can also include a stable currency and things such as uniform weights and measures and free exchange within the territory they control.

Ruling classes by their nature have a mixed view of innovation and the economic growth it creates. On the one hand this is welcome: it creates more wealth for them to tax, and rents that they can spend on things such as palaces, impressive public works and lavish living (and above all on their favourite pastime, wars). However, it is also a threat to them. They are at the top of the existing social hierarchy so why should they welcome change, particularly if their position is insecure? In addition, innovation and the greater wealth it brings to ordinary people and members of the productive classes weaken the ruling classes' control over them and give them greater autonomy and freedom of action. This is why throughout history ruling groups have often supported the anti-innovation institutions of the moral economy by enforcing their norms and rules through courts or by measures such as statutory privileges given to institutions such as guilds. This means deliberately preventing technological or business or financial innovations. Here another factor comes into play: those who have succeeded in the world of voluntary production and exchange and thereby acquired wealth often fear that they will lose that wealth to ambitious younger upstarts and so they turn to the political power, the ruling classes, to protect their own position and entrench it against further change. In the most extreme cases, ruling groups deliberately and systematically stop or reverse innovation.

We can see these other forces at work in all of the previous episodes of innovation but particularly in the Chinese case. There the Song dynasty was overthrown and China conquered in 1276—by the Mongols. This by itself did not bring an end to the dynamism of Chinese society as the Mongol Yuan dynasty did not make major institutional changes and was also increasingly ineffective. The subsequent Han Chinese dynasty, the Ming, which came to power in 1368 in the person of the

Hongwu emperor, reacted to the Mongol conquest by deliberately reversing the policy of the Song and seeking to reduce the commercialisation of Chinese society and to arrest or even roll back innovation of all kinds. The most dramatic example of the latter was the ban on building ships that could sail long distances out of sight of land, which came into effect towards the end of the fifteenth century. Special privileges were given to merchant cartels, with the deliberate aim of stabilising the Chinese economy and society, i.e. limiting innovation. Towards the end of the dynasty, incapacity on the part of the last Ming emperors meant that many of these rules were not enforced and China became once again a very dynamic and mercantile society, but in 1645 the Manchus conquered China and founded the Qing dynasty. The first four Qing emperors were able and conscientious rulers and they restored the earlier policy of the Ming in this regard.

So although innovation is indeed produced by the

interaction of ordinary people through the institutions of trade and exchange, and although many innovations do require other innovations to have been made previously before they become possible (so giving the innovative process a cumulative quality), it does not follow that the explosion of innovation that we call modernity was inevitable and could not have happened earlier than it did. The evidence suggests that although almost certainly particular factors had to be in place or reach a critical level before modern innovation could happen, those conditions had been met long before the eighteenth century. Moreover, the key question is that of why the innovative spurt that began in northwestern Europe in the eighteenth century did not fade away like earlier ones but was sustained and indeed accelerated. In that case the force of innovation was able to overcome the social institutions and ruling classes that had choked off sustained innovation in earlier periods. Why was this?

Explaining Europe's take-off

If Ridley's account of innovation and the innovative process is correct (which I think it is) then that itself gives us ideas as to what the answer to that question might be. In broad terms it is that social interactions and relations based upon trade and exchange became more powerful and widespread than those based upon power and also social institutions that reflected a fear of change. Societies went from being predominantly *neophobic* to predominantly *neophiliac*.

There were three specific changes. Firstly some ruling classes (or more accurately enough members of some ruling classes to make a difference) became supportive of innovation and employed political power to

175

assist it by sweeping away social and legal barriers to it (Mokyr 2011, 2018). Secondly there was the emergence of coalitions of social interests that were aware that they gained from innovation and voluntary action. Between roughly 1770 and 1860 they were engaged in an often fierce political and social/cultural conflict with a coalition of interests that opposed innovations and the changes they brought —this second group included both some elites and members of the lower classes, particularly peasants and traditional artisans. In most places it was the forces that favoured innovation that triumphed (although they disagreed among themselves over what led to it and how to encourage it while controlling it). Thirdly there was a cultural shift in which innovation and enterprise came to be admired and emulated, rather than being feared and deprecated (McCloskey 2007, 2010, 2017). (There are several theories as to why these three things came to be strong enough to overcome the countervailing forces when and where they did, but we do not have space to explore those here.)

This is far from bringing the argument to an end, however. In the first place it raises the big question of whether the process of innovation that Ridley identifies is as beneficial as he thinks it is—there are many who disagree with him. More seriously, we must ask whether this time it really is different. Will the sustained and accelerating innovation we have seen for the last two hundred years or so continue, perhaps to the point of a so-called singularity after which things will swiftly become so different that we cannot even imagine or describe what they will be like? Alternatively, are there reasons to think that the emphasis on innovation is overblown and that we are only living in the longest and most dramatic episode of innovation yet, which will end and fade away like all the others? Perhaps most pressingly, could we accidentally and unintentionally recreate the conditions and incentives that applied for most of human history and so bring innovation to an end that way?

Arguments against innovation

The first question is actually the easiest to deal with in some ways. Ever since the very start of modernity there have been people who have decried innovation and particularly technological innovation. One common theme is a focus on the costs of creative destruction (the destruction part such as the disappearance of livelihoods and occupations because of innovation) while ignoring the creative part (the new and different products, occupations and ways of living that appear as a result of those innovations). The more profound argument is that there is something inherently wrong with the process of sustained innovation and the world it has created. The position of the radical critics is that sustained innovation is in some sense impious because it disrupts a natural order and creates a way of living that runs against our nature as living creatures. The conclusion is that it will have catastrophic ecological and social consequences unless it is arrested and then reversed.

The response to this kind of argument is straightforward: it is empirically false. As Ridley argues and authors such as Julian Lincoln Simon have shown, the effect of technological innovation has been and continues to be to reduce the impact of human beings on the environment. The pattern is for an older way of doing things to be enhanced by innovation and pushed to a limit and scale where it does indeed start to have an adverse impact. At that point, however, the tinkering and exchange-based process that Ridley describes leads to further innovation that resolves the problem. A current example is farming, particularly livestock farming, which is having a negative impact on the biosphere but looks set to be replaced almost entirely, due to innovations such as the development of cultured meat. As far as human well-being is concerned, the obvious rejoinder is that in most cases technophobes and neo-luddites do not show any enthusiasm for abandoning the results of innovation in their own life (with some honourable exceptions). The overwhelming majority of people everywhere would choose innovation and its results over the life of their ancestors.

Are innovation and growth sustainable?

A different argument is that innovation has brought great benefits but that it and the world we live in are unsustainable and will not continue. The usual case here is that innovation and growth cannot continue indefinitely because of the physical limits of the world. While true in extremis, most of the arguments in this vein are again refuted by the facts. Moreover, as the lecture points out, the key resource for innovation is knowledge and ideas and the way these are combined and recombined as a result of human interaction. This is so large as to be near infinite as far as we are concerned. The more serious argument relates to one resource in particular, energy, or more precisely usable energy and above all fossil fuels.

The thesis here is that the growth we have seen in the modern world is not the result of innovation but rather because of humanity having made use of the accumulated energy in fossil fuels. In this view, to the extent that we have higher levels of innovation now, this is a consequence of economic growth rather than a cause. (The further argument is that there was extensive innovation in the past without this leading to growth— the missing ingredient was energy.) The problem with this view is not that we will ever physically run out of fossil fuels or energy. Rather the challenge is that with time it takes ever increasing amounts of energy to get oil in particular out of the ground. This is measured by the EROEI (energy returned on energy invested) ratio. In the early part of the twentieth century it took the energy equivalent of one barrel of oil to get nearly a hundred actual barrels of oil out of the ground, but that ratio is now around one to twenty and declining. The common argument that we can simply replace fossil fuels with other, renewable, energy sources is rejected on two grounds. Firstly, the EROEI of renewables is too low to support a complex industrial civilisation (once the energy costs of producing things such as wind turbines and solar panels are taken into account) and there are theoretical reasons why this will not change. Secondly, there are things that can be done with petroleum in particular that cannot be done with any renewable energy because the latter is too diffuse and hard to store—oil by contrast contains a large amount of usable energy in a very light and compact form.

If this is true then modern growth will slowly come to an end, regardless of how much innovation there is, and we will revert to the historical norm (over a period of about seventy to two hundred years—most of the authors who take this view think that the process has already begun) (Greer 2017, 2019). As growth declines, and with it trade and exchange, so will innovation, which will also return to the historically normal pattern. This argument deserves to be taken seriously and its critique of renewable energy is pointed and effective, given current technology. The point, however, is that we can actually see what kind of innovation it is that we need to resolve this challenge: a means of storing, transporting and most of all compressing usable energy, from whatever source (a super battery if you will). If the model of innovation as a process presented by Matt Ridley is correct, then unless something else changes we should expect to see innovations that will do this happen in the way that he describes, by many piecemeal changes brought about by the interaction of large numbers of people (as he says, we are already seeing significant development in battery technology). Of course, it is possible that this will not happen, perhaps because the necessary innovations and discoveries will not happen in time. In that case our future is indeed bleak. However, the chances are that the innovation will happen—so long as other factors do not change in ways that hamper the innovative process.

Has innovation slowed down?

A different argument that has been made by a number of economists and others is that innovation actually peaked some time ago and that there are structural reasons for this. This argument was made by Jonathan Huebner in 2005 and has been elaborated by others, notably Tyler Cowen, Theodore Modis and Robert James Gordon (Huebner 2005; Cowen 2011; Modis 2002; Gordon 2000). The argument here is that the pace of innovation as measured by a number of indices has slowed down significantly in the last thirty to forty years. This is held to explain the definite decline in growth rates in developed economies since the 1970s. According to this view the peak of innovation or at least of innovations that led to significant changes in productivity took place in the later nineteenth and early twentieth century. Since then, the argument goes, we have been basically filling in the gaps and refining those earlier fundamental breakthroughs. Much of this work, particularly by Modis, is aimed at the arguments of authors such as Hans Moravec (1990) and Raymond Kurzweil (2006) that we are actually seeing accelerating innovation, which will lead us to a technological singularity in the near future (as mentioned earlier). The argument of the sceptics is that innovation, like most processes, is self-limiting and typically follows an S-shaped curve. Initially there is an accelerating rate of invention and innovation but the pace of innovation gradually slows and eventually flattens out. The commonest explanation for this cites one of the phenomena that Matt Ridley discusses in his lecture. Innovation leads to increased specialisation (as time is freed up so that, for example, we no longer need to have

80 per cent of the working population tied up in farming) and an increasingly elaborate division of labour. In other words, it leads to a higher level of social complexity. The problem in this view is that this greater complexity eventually makes effective innovation more difficult because it raises the cost of making the crucial personal and intellectual connections. In that case innovation is indeed an ultimately self-limiting process or at least one that has lengthy pauses.

The question of whether or not innovation has actually slowed down is actually a difficult one to resolve, because much of the debate is qualitative rather than purely quantitative. The argument is not simply that there are fewer patents, but rather that the innovations we are now getting are relatively trivial and not life transforming or productivity enhancing in the way that earlier ones such as electricity and the internal combustion engine were. There are two responses to this. This first is that it is simply too soon to tell if many of the more recent innovations will have as big an effect as those earlier ones or not. One of the main points that Matt Ridley makes in his lecture is precisely relevant here: we tend to systematically overestimate the impact of innovation in the short run and underestimate its long-run impact. This kind of argument gets support in the work of David Edgerton (2019), particularly his book *The Shock of the Old: Technology and Global History Since 1900*. At first sight this looks like the antithesis to the case made by Ridley, as he argues that in histories of technology novelty is exaggerated while we overlook the persistence and staying power of older established techniques and technologies and even the revival in some cases of previously abandoned technologies. As he says, popular magazines are full of technologies and innovations that were meant to happen and transform the world but did not, while very old technologies continue without people noticing. The picture he paints, however, is very much in line with that of Ridley. Innovation is not a matter of heroic inventors or major transformative breakthroughs as much as a process of piecemeal changes brought about by tinkering and trial and error by individuals—the role of largescale research and development is overestimated—and it is the cumulative effect of all of these individually minor changes and marginal improvements that is transformative. Most innovations fail, often because while technically feasible they are economically too costly or because they try to combine incompatible functions (supersonic passenger transport is an example of the former, flying cars of the latter). This means that the process of innovation is both fast and slow in the modern world: fast because ideas and experiments take place in ever larger numbers and at a higher frequency; slow because it takes time for the small changes to add up to something radical.

The other response to the alleged slowing down of innovation is that this is real but is not due to an endogenous factor such as the feedback effects of the greater complexity produced by innovation. Rather it is because of political and social changes. This argument has great force and relates directly to one of the main points of Ridley's lecture and perhaps the greatest threat facing the innovative process of modernity today.

Major threats to innovation and growth

Given what Ridley argues about the social basis of innovation and so ultimately of intensive growth and the modern world, then ideas and beliefs or public policies or laws that hinder that process or even stop it can have the (probably unintended) result of stopping innovation. If, as I argue, the sustained innovation of modernity was not the inevitable result of certain factors reaching a critical level but only happened because other structural forces that had previously prevented that kind of take-off were overcome, then it is perfectly possible that either deliberately or inadvertently we will bring about a return to the historical norm. The last two and a half centuries of sustained innovation and growth will indeed be just another episode of a much longer history.

There are three kinds of dynamic that might do this. The first is the effect of laws and institutions that are in theory designed to encourage innovation but which, given the understanding of it presented here, will actually choke it off. The main example of this, which Ridley cites, is intellectual property (IP). In theory patents and copyright are supposed to encourage risky innovation by granting the inventor a time-limited monopoly which will yield a monopoly rent (super normal income). There are many problems with this, to put it mildly. Quite apart from the philosophical problem that property rights are a response to the scarcity of resources and the conflicts this gives rise to, whereas information is an abundant non-scarce resource, there are practical difficulties. The major empirical problem is that there is no clear evidence that historically patents have encouraged productive innovation. The theory presented by Ridley leads in fact to the opposite conclusion, that they hamper innovation. If innovation is the product of the exchange of ideas and the efforts of enterprising individuals to improve or adapt things that others have done before them, then anything that makes this process more costly or drawn out, or in extremis prevents it entirely, will block innovation. In terms of the present, the evidence is strong that the kind of intellectual property regime advocated and enforced by the US in particular hampers innovation through the copying and improvement of existing technology. It also provides ample opportunities for rent seeking in the shape of patent trolls who use patents simply as a means to raise income through vexatious lawsuits, and creates a class of IP rentiers who gain wealth and income not by innovation but through the monopoly they have been granted by the state. In addition, IP increasingly undermines real property rights in actual physical commodities by limiting the use their owners can make of them in all kinds of intrusive ways—this also hinders innovation.

The second problem is that of attitudes, ideas and beliefs and the politics they give rise to in modern democracies. The challenge here is the persistence of fear and unease about innovation and the change it brings, which leads to pressure from two sources for measures that will slow down or stop particular innovations or even the innovation in general. The first comes from people who have indeed lost out from the effects of particular innovations or who believe that they have lost even when that is not true. The second is from people who have gained from previous innovations or the existing state of affairs and fear that continuing innovations will undermine their position. Together these two kinds of pressure, one from threatened elites, the other from a wider popular movement, can produce a very powerful politics that deliberately tries to slow down change or to prevent it entirely. We can see this for example in resistance to 'sharing economy' applications such as

Uber. Much contemporary politics, such as resistance to migration or support for protectionism, ultimately reflects a fear of innovation and change and a focus upon costs and losers from change rather than benefits and gainers. In addition, there are a number of ideas that have become very influential and which reflect this outlook. One of the most powerful, which Ridley discusses, is that of the precautionary principle, the idea that we should not have innovation until we are sure that an innovation will not have harmful effects. Since we can never be certain of that, this is in practice and if taken seriously a call for no change or innovation of any kind. In addition, because in many cases not doing anything or not innovating is itself risky, the argument is incoherent and does not provide a real guide to action. To the extent that it influences political debate, however, it can have very harmful effects. (The contrary view is the 'proactionary principle' that we should try to identify problems and challenges as early as possible so that the innovative process can produce solutions to them sooner.)

However, the biggest problem is the third one. Bad institutions such as intellectual property and politics motivated by a misguided fear of innovation can do harm, but they cannot now stop the innovative process unless they operate on a worldwide scale. If they do not, the process will continue in those parts of the world less affected by them. So, although there may be parts of the planet that stagnate the world as a whole will not. In addition, the parts of the world that do go down the route of arresting innovation will fall behind those that do not, by a number of measures, and eventually this will become insupportable. However, there is a development that threatens to create a global check to innovation. This is the growth of supranational regulatory regimes such as the EU, and the global network of harmonised regulations created by so-called trade deals. Although such deals are intended to promote trade and exchange by removing what are called non-tariff barriers to trade (essentially, conflicting regulatory regimes that prevent products being freely traded across regulatory borders), they do so by harmonising regulatory regimes. This creates an increasingly global and standardised pattern of regulation.

This is very dangerous for the innovative process because it threatens to revive the incentives facing rulers that were described earlier, but this time on a global scale. One of the main reasons why some ruling classes eventually supported innovation instead of trying to check it was the reality that they faced of being in competition with other elites that controlled other parts of the planet's surface. They could only enforce regulations in the geographical areas that they controlled and to do so at a high level disadvantaged them in the competition. In addition, for the greater part of modern history (up until the 1930s or even the 1950s) regulation was fairly light and general in content rather than specific and detailed. Now it is huge in scope, enormous in volume, and amazingly detailed and precise. What this does in a whole range of areas (pharmaceuticals being only the most glaring example) is to restrict the innovative process and create barriers to the kinds of trade and exchange that drive it.

However, trying to resolve this by removing the clash of regulations and with it the competition between regulatory regimes is to fall into what we may call the trap of empire. Empires that unite a large part of the world create an extensive area of stable government and exchange. Initially this creates more exchange and economic dynamism. However, the incentives for the rulers of the empire to control and check innovation are extremely powerful and they no longer need to fear competition from other elites in the way that rulers of smaller states do. The current trend is to create something like a global regulatory order, a kind of world empire in fact. This would surely stop innovation in its tracks and restore the incentives and conditions that led popular processes and elite action to check innovation for most of recorded history.

Matt Ridley explains clearly what innovation is, what it derives from, and the benefits it has brought. He also sets out some of the dangers we now face, both political and cultural, and institutional. However, I fear he is still too optimistic. To think that the modern world of innovation is natural or inevitable is to fail to realise how contingent it is and how much its appearance was the outcome of chance events. We should not take it for granted and we should be always aware of the constant danger that often well-meaning moves, along with the influence of mistaken ideas and sentiments, will bring it to a halt and restore the world of our ancestors.

[1]   Cowen, T. (2004) *Creative Destruction: How Globalization Is Changing the World's Cultures.* Princeton University Press.

[2]   Cowen, T. (2011) *The Great Stagnation: How America Ate All of the Low Hanging Fruit of Modern History, Got Sick, and Will (Eventually) Feel Better.* New York: Penguin.

[3]   Davies, S. J. (2019) *The Wealth Explosion: The Nature and Origins of Modernity.* Brighton: Edward Everett Root.

[4]   Edgerton, D. (2019) *The Shock of the Old: Technology and Global History Since 1900.* London: Profile.

[5]   Edwards, R. A. (2013) Redefining industrial revolution: Song China and England (https://economicdynamics.org/meetpapers/2013/paper_351.pdf).

[6]   Goldstone, J. A. (2002) Efflorescences and economic growth in world history: rethinking the 'rise of the West' and the Industrial Revolution. *Journal of World History* 13(2): 323–89.

[7]   Gordon, R. J. (2000) Does the 'new economy' measure up to the great inventions of the past? *Journal of Economic Perspectives* 14(4): 49–74.

[8]   Greer, J. M. (2017) *The Retro Future: Looking to the Past to Reinvent the Future.* Gabriola Island, BC: New Society Publishers.

[9]   Greer, J. M. (2019) *The Long Descent: A User's Guide to the End of the Industrial Age.* Danville, IL: Founders House Publishing.

[10] Huebner, J. (2005) A possible declining trend for worldwide innovation. *Technological Forecasting and Social Change* 72(8): 980–86.

[11] Kaczynski, T. J. (2016) *Anti-Tech Revolution: Why and How.* Scottsdale, AZ: Fitch and Madison.

[12] Kaczynski, T. J. (2018) [1995] *Industrial Society and Its Future.* Pub House Books.

[13] Kealey, T. (1996) *The Economic Laws of Scientific Research.* London: Palgrave Macmillan.

[14] Kurzweil, R. (2006) *The Singularity Is Near.* London: Duckworth.

[15] McCloskey, D. (2007) *The Bourgeois Virtues: Ethics for an Age of Commerce.* Chicago University Press.

[16] McCloskey, D. (2010) *Bourgeois Dignity: Why Economics Can't Explain the Modern World.* Chicago University Press.

[17] McCloskey, D. (2017) *Bourgeois Equality: How Ideas, Not Capital or Institutions Enriched the World.* Chicago University Press.

[18] Modis, T. (2002) The limits of complexity and change. *The Futurist* May–June, pp. 26–32.

[19] Mokyr, J. (2011) *The Enlightened Economy: Britain and the Industrial Revolution, 1700–1850.* London: Penguin.

[20] Mokyr, J. (2018) *A Culture of Growth: The Origins of the Modern Economy.* Princeton University Press.

[21] Moravec, H. (1990) *Mind Children: The Future of Robot and Human Intelligence.* Harvard University Press.

[22] Rustow, D. A. (1980) *Freedom and Power: A Historical Critique of Civilisation.* Princeton University Press.

[23] Scott, J. C. (1976) *The Moral Economy of the Peasant: Rebellion and Subsistence in Southeast Asia.* Princeton University Press.

[24] Thompson, E. P. (1991) *Customs in Common.* New York: New Press.

[25] Ward-Perkins, B. (2006) *The Fall of Rome and the End of Civilisation.* Oxford University Press.

关于经济事务研究所
（IEA）

　　该研究所是一家有担保限制的研究和教育慈善机构（编号CC 235 351）。其使命是通过分析和阐述市场在解决经济和社会问题方面的作用，增进对自由社会基本制度的理解。

　　经济事务研究所通过以下方式履行自己的使命：

- 高质量的出版计划
- 会议、研讨会、讲座和其他活动
- 面向中小学生和大学生的外联活动
- 安排媒体见面

　　经济事务研究所由已故的安东尼·费希尔爵士（Antony Fisher）于1955年创立，是一个教育慈善机构，而非政治组织。它独立于任何政党或团体，不在任何选举、全民投票或任何其他时间进行旨在影响任何政党或候选人的支持率的活动。它的经费来自出版物销售、会议费用和自愿捐款。

除了自身主要的系列出版物之外，经济事务研究所还与白金汉大学合作出版《经济事务》（Economic Affairs）杂志。

经济事务研究所的工作得到一个杰出的国际学术顾问委员会和一个杰出的荣誉研究员小组的协助。他们与其他学者一起，对经济事务研究所未来的出版物进行评审，他们的评估采用匿名方式。因此，经济事务研究所的所有论文都要经过与顶尖学术期刊同样严格的独立评审程序。

经济事务研究所的出版物在中学和大学中得到广泛使用。它们还在世界各地销售和重印，并经常被翻译成多种语言。

自1974年以来，经济事务研究所帮助建立了一个由70多个国家的100家类似机构组成的全球网络。它们都是独立的，但承担着经济事务研究所的使命。

经济事务研究所出版物中表达的观点是作者的观点，而不是该研究所（没有企业观点）、其董事会成员、学术咨询委员会成员或高级职员的观点。

本研究所衷心感谢已故教授罗纳德·科斯（Ronald Coase）为本研究所的出版计划和其他工作在财务方面给予的慷慨支持。